Foundations

of

Freedom

a Living History of our Bill of Rights

Foundations

of

Freedom

By

John H. Rhodehamel

Stephen F. Rohde

Paul Von Blum

Constitutional Rights Foundation

Bill of Rights
BICENTENNIAL

Harry L. Usher, President
Constitutional Rights Foundation

Raymond C. Fisher, Chairman
Constitutional Rights Foundation
Bill of Rights Bicentennial Committee

Jerome C. Byrne, Chairman
Constitutional Rights Foundation
Publications Committee

EDITOR AND CONTENT DESIGN
Marshall Croddy

Chapters I-VI were written by John Rhodehamel; Chapters VII, VIII, XI-XIV were written by Stephen F Rohde; Chapters IX-XII were written by Paul Von Blum. Marshall Croddy wrote "John Marshall and the Power of Judicial Review," and the Preface.

REVIEWERS
Jerome C. Byrne, CRF Publications Committee
Justice Ronald George, CRF Publications Committee
Lloyd M. Smith, CRF Publications Committee
Marjorie Steinberg, CRF Publications Committee

PRINCIPAL STAFF
Todd Clark, Executive Director
Kathleen Kirby, Education Director
Vivian Monroe, Director, Bill of Rights Celebration Project
Tina M. Esposito, Senior Associate Publications Manager
Suzan Sherburn, Copy Editor
Amy Gordon, Publications Assistant

PRODUCTION
Gerry Rosentswieg/The Graphics Studio, Design
Lanning Gold, Photo Research
Taurus, Inc., Typesetting
Navigator Press, Printing

Constitutional Rights Foundation
601 South Kingsley Drive
Los Angeles, California 90005
(213) 487-5590

ACKNOWLEDGEMENTS
The development of these materials was financially assisted through a generous grant from the W.M. Keck Foundation.

We gratefully acknowledge the Huntington Library for its contributions of original manuscripts, rare books and other documents presented in this book.

We gratefully acknowledge the following sources for photographs, documents, and letters, which were used with permission.

PHOTOGRAPHS
AP/Wide World Newsphotos: 84 (McCarthy), 87 (March on D.C.).

AP/Wide World Photos: 8 (Poster), 15, 24, 26 (Buddhist monk), 28,31 (Kent State), 34 (NRA seal), (Lennon Paper), 35 (Kent State), 55 (Dr. King leads march), 62 (Susan B. Anthony), 65 (anti-war [below]), 77, 79, 81 (Zoot Suit), 88, 93, 96 (Electric Chair), 97, 105 (Warren Court) (Bork).

The Bettmann Archive, New York, N.Y.: 9 (Drinking Fountain), 19 (below), 21, 24, 25 (Williams portrait), 26, 34 (gun makers), 49 (Milliken's Bend) (Confederate officers), 52, 53 (Mosley), 55 (Union soldiers), 58 (sweat shop), 60 (Chinese workers), 62, 65 (song), 68 (Holmes portrait), 73 (Dust Bowl refugees), 78 (Mochida's), 80 (100th Infantry), 81 (WWII Victory Celebration), 99 (Amish) (Church), 101 (Mosque) (Church).

UPI/Bettmann Newsphotos: 11 (Speaker), 16 (King John), 66 (McCarthy), 75 (Sanger Portrait) (Abortion Confrontation), 78 (Manzanar Camp), 84 (Hollywood Writers), 85, 88 (KKK), 91, 92, 104 (NRA).

UPI/Bettmann: 8 (KKK), 10 (KKK), 11 (Demonstrators), 32 (Nixon), 39 (Ted Koppel), 53 (lunch counter), 55 (protester), 56, 61 (Rosa Parks), 63 (parade 1915) (parade 1976), 64 (protesters), 65 (anti-war [above]), 66 , 71 (Republic Steel), 72 (Gitlow), 73 , 74, 78 (Japanese Americans being searched), 80 (Korematsu et al),86, 92 (Marshall portrait), 95, 96, 99 (High School) (Hare Krishna), 101 (horse), 103, 106, 107 (Book Burning) (Art supporters), 108 (Abortion Demonstration).

Reuters/Bettmann Newsphotos: 109.

Reuters/Bettmann: 19 (above), 20 (Poll tax), 32 (poll tax), 102 (Priest) (Evangelist).

The Steven Heller Collection: 60 (racial caricatures), 66, 68 (patriotic appeals), 72 (1930s magazine), 73 (Mother Earth), 76 (poster), 104 (poster).

The Henry E. Huntington Library and Art Gallery, San Marino, CA: 9 (Federal Hall), 15, 16, 18, 20, 22, 23, 25, 27, 30, 31 (Boston Massacre), 32, 34, 36, 39, 40, 41, 42, 45, 46, 47, 49, 51, 60.

Japanese American Library, San Francisco, CA: 76 (1942 poster).

Library of Congress, Washington, D.C.: 10 (troops), 12, 44, 48 (Justice Marshall), 55 (Slavery's end), 58 (Boy), 59, 63, 69, 70 (Federal agent) (Temperance).

Mark Taper Forum Press, Los Angeles, CA: 81 (Zoot Suit).

National Portrait Gallery, Smithsonian Institute, Washington, D.C.: 33, 37, 38, 48 (Marshall portrait), 50, 53 (Taney portrait), 57 (Douglass portrait), 68 (Holmes/Vanity Fair).

Photo Researchers, Inc. NYC: 8 (voters), 24, 82, 102 (Indianpeace), 108 (Voting).

Gerry Rosentswieg Collection: 60 (Racist images), 71 (Flappers), 87 (American artists), 107 (Button).

Wheatley Press, Inc, Los Angeles, CA: 77 (poster).

NEWS HEADLINES AND POLITICAL CARTOONS
Los Angeles Times: 55 (headline), 70 (cartoon), 73, 76, 79, 88, 91.

Long Island Press: 83.

Reprinted by permission:
Tribune Media Service: 96 (Dale Locher cartoon).

Reprinted with permission from the Chicago Sun-Times: 107 (Bill Mauldin cartoon).

Printed by permission of the Norman Rockwell Family Trust Copyright © 1964 the Norman Rockwell Family Trust: 90. Printed by permission of Dayton Daily News: 63 (Mike Peters cartoon).

This book is dedicated to
Jerome C. Byrne and Lloyd M. Smith
who as the long-time Chairman and Senior Member of
the Constitutional Rights Foundation Publications
Committee have made incalculable contributions to
education about the Bill of Rights.

FOUNDATIONS OF FREEDOM:
a Living History of our Bill of Rights

FOREWORD

Two hundred years ago, the United States ratified the Bill of Rights. These first ten amendments to the Constitution promised Americans a level of personal liberty and freedom from governmental interference unparalleled anywhere on the globe. The product of nearly 800 years of evolutionary political and legal development, the ideas embodied in the amendments are a high water mark in western thought. For two centuries, our Bill of Rights has shined out as a beacon drawing to our shores millions seeking its light. Millions more have been inspired by it to achieve the same standards in their own homelands. By any measure, the Bill of Rights is one of America's greatest achievements.

In essence, the Bill of Rights stands for the restraint of governmental power, the protection of minority rights against majoritarian interests, and the dignity of the individual. Emboldened by the amendments adopted after the great Civil War, the 13th, 14th and 15th, and subsequent amendments, it also embodies the values of fairness, toleration of diversity and equal treatment under the law.

The history of the Bill of Rights is the history of the United States. As the history of the Republic is unfinished so is that of the Bill of Rights. Largely ignored in the early years of nation building, the Bill of Rights was rediscovered in our own century as those who believed in its promise fought for recognition: women, African Americans, Latinos, Asian Americans, and the first inhabitants of our country, Native Americans. As we approach a new century and millennium, other groups

Essay

8

have made similar claims on the basis of age, sexual orientation or special physical needs. It remains to be seen whether the document, crafted so long ago and invigorated by subsequent amendments, will fulfill these hopes.

The story of the Bill of Rights encompasses both triumph and tragedy. Its doctrines have been sorely tested in times of war or national crisis. In these dark times, we as a nation have strayed from its meaning, succumbing to the fears of the moment or to ancient prejudices and have denied to others the rights we ourselves so jealously guard.

Above all, the story of the Bill of Rights is about people. Some are heros who dedicated their lives or who risked everything to make real the ideals they saw embodied in the Bill of Rights. Some are jurists or scholars whose ideas carried on the traditions and debates started by the Founders. Others found themselves in situations which, through fate or design, influenced the development of rights which benefited everyone. Some are not heros at all. Instead, they were society's outcasts or criminals whose cases carved out new rights or protection against the power of government.

FEDERAL HALL
The Seat of CONGRESS

FOR COLORED ONLY

concerning toleration

9

By its nature, the Bill of Rights will never be finished. Article V of the Constitution gives each generation the right to alter the fabric of government according to its own lights and to meet the needs of a changing America. The U.S. Supreme Court, exercising its power of judicial review, will continue to interpret the meanings of the Bill of Rights and apply them to modern realities. Proponents of change, representing the full spectrum of politics, will always use the doctrines of the Bill of Rights as a shield for advocacy and as a sword to prick the conscience of society.

The original copy of the Bill of Rights, along with the Constitution and the Declaration of Independence, can be found sealed in helium and protected by bullet-proof glass in the rotunda of the National

KENNED

Assassin Flees

Archives in Washington D.C. There resides the body, its spirit moves elsewhere. It hovers over our churches and synagogues and mosques. It sparks arguments in bars and diners and schools, in public parks and court rooms, and in the halls of Congress. It finds expression in enduring issues: press versus privacy, law and order versus the rights of the accused, majority interests versus minority needs. It follows the police officer on the streets and visits the condemned on death row. It stalks the stages of rock and roll concerts or darkened movie theaters, and fills the pens and brushes of writers and artists.

It is carried on placards for a thousand causes and screamed by angry voices. It watches over the shoulders of voters as they cast their ballots or employers as they interview job seekers. It moves across the face of America and inspires the hearts of the people. Like no other document of state, it binds us together, while at the same time dividing us in its meaning. It is what America is all about.

To this spirit, *Foundations of Freedom* is dedicated. As Constitutional Rights Foundation's commemorative publication in celebration of the bicentennial of the Bill of Rights, we hope it will link the past to the present, and help all Americans embrace the Bill of Rights as a living document essential to everyday life and to the future. While we celebrate our heritage, it is also a perfect time to rededicate ourselves to its message of toleration and fairness for all and to the education of our young people in the rights and responsibilities of enlightened citizenship.

Original Bill of Rights, 1789.

1ST AMENDMENT	Congress shall make no law respecting an establishment of religion, or prohibiting the free exercise thereof; or abridging the freedom of speech, or of the press, or the right of the people peaceably to assemble, and to petition the Government for a redress of grievances.
2ND AMENDMENT	A well regulated Militia, being necessary to the security of a free State, the right of the people to keep and bear Arms, shall not be infringed.
3RD AMENDMENT	No Soldier shall, in time of peace be quartered in any house, without the consent of the Owner, nor in time of war, but in a manner to be prescribed by law.
4TH AMENDMENT	The right of the people to be secure in their persons, houses, papers, and effects, against unreasonable searches and seizures, shall not be violated, and no Warrants shall issue, but upon probable cause, supported by Oath or affirmation, and particularly describing the place to be searched, and the persons or things to seized.
5TH AMENDMENT	No person shall be held to answer for a capital, or otherwise infamous crime, unless on a presentment or indictment of a Grand Jury, except in cases arising in the land or naval forces, or in the Militia, when in actual service in time of War or public danger; nor shall any person be subject for the same offence to be twice put in jeopardy of life or limb, nor shall be compelled in any criminal case to be a witness against himself, nor be deprived of life, liberty, or property, without due process of law; nor shall private property be taken for public use without just compensation.
6TH AMENDMENT	In all criminal prosecutions, the accused shall enjoy the right to a speedy and public trial, by an impartial jury of the State and district wherein the crime shall have been committed; which district shall have been previously ascertained by law, and to be informed of the nature and cause of the accusation; to be confronted with the witnesses against him; to have compulsory process for obtaining witnesses in his favor, and to have the Assistance of Counsel for his defence.
7TH AMENDMENT	In suits at common law, where the value in controversy shall exceed twenty dollars, the right of trial by jury shall be preserved, and no fact tried by a jury shall be otherwise re-examined in any Court of the United States, than according to the rules of the common law.
8TH AMENDMENT	Excessive bail shall not be required, nor excessive fines imposed, nor cruel and unusual punishments inflicted.
9TH AMENDMENT	The enumeration in the Constitution of certain rights shall not be construed to deny or disparage others retained by the people.
10TH AMENDMENT	The powers not delegated to the United States by the Constitution, nor prohibited by it to the States, are reserved to the States respectively, or to the people.
13TH AMENDMENT (1865)	Neither slavery nor involuntary servitude, except as a punishment for crime whereof the party shall have been duly convicted, shall exist within the United States, or any place subject to their jurisdiction.
14TH AMENDMENT (1868)	All persons born or naturalized in the United States and subject to the jurisdiction thereof, are citizens of the United States and of the State wherein they reside. No State shall make or enforce any law which shall abridge the privileges or immunities of citizens of the United States; nor shall any State deprive any person of life, liberty, or property, without due process of law; nor deny to any person within its jurisdiction the equal protection of the laws.
15TH AMENDMENT (1870)	The right of citizens of the United States to vote shall not be denied or abridged by the United States or by any State on account of race, color, or previous condition of servitude.
19TH AMENDMENT (1920)	The right of citizens of the United States to vote shall not be denied or abridged by the United States or by any State on account of sex.

ORIGINS

The growth of a tradition of individual liberties protected against government oppression can be traced back to a series of important state documents in British history. The tradition of liberty is the choicest gift of the English-speaking people. It began in 1215 with the Magna Carta and was confirmed by subsequent monarchs and expanded by other statutes. It includes the Petition of Rights of 1628 which served as the opening gun of the final battle between Parliament and the Crown for control of the government of Britain. This contest ended with the Bill of Rights in 1689, marking Parliament's victory over the Crown in the "Glorious Revolution." From there, the scene shifts to America, where the British tradition would find new expression in the revolt against Britain, and in the Declaration of Independence, the United States Constitution and the Bill of Rights.

In spite of the importance of these documents in British constitutional history, much of what we call "the British Constitution" remains unwritten. It is a collection—although not collected in any single source—of laws passed by Parliament, of charters granted by kings and queens, of decisions in the courts, and the practices of England's ancient, but ever-changing, body of common law. This assortment of precedents and enactments, which had grown alongside the nation itself, made for a useful vagueness as to exactly what the Constitution meant. It could be what the British wanted it to be, within the limits defined by the broad principles they had agreed upon.

The recurring theme of the story that began with Magna Carta is always the struggle to assert the rights of the people against the arbitrary power of the Crown. No chapter of that story is more important than the 17th-century battle between Parliament and the monarchy for mastery of the governance of Britain. That battle consumed a good part of the century. The clear lesson, in both Britain and America, was that only representative government could assure that the liberties of the people would be safeguarded and extended.

As the 17th century began, the most celebrated of English dynasties came to an end with the death in 1603 of the last Tudor monarch, the great Queen Elizabeth. The crown of England passed into the hands of the Stuarts of Scotland, a headstrong and stubborn race of kings. The first of the line, James I, ruled from 1603 to 1625. He was succeeded by his son, Charles I. The father quarreled over money with Parliament and dissolved it several times. The son's far more violent feudings with Parliament plunged England into its greatest civil war and caused the King himself to lose his head. Although religious differences were the root cause of much of the strife, it was money that first brought the Stuarts into conflict with Parliament.

Not long after becoming king, Charles had his country entangled in war with Spain and France. War is always an expensive proposition and Parliament was in no mood to pay. It was for refusing to approve taxes to cover the war costs that the King dissolved the first two Parliaments of his reign. He also resorted to a forced loan, with the threat of prison held over those who refused to pay. This enactment challenged two of Magna Carta's great principles—that of taxation only through the consent of the people's representatives and of the right to due process of the law. In 1627 Parliament countered with the Petition of Rights.

Modern tax protesters reflect ancient debates.

Kings: Genealogical history of the kings of England, manuscript on parchment, dated about 1465.

This 500-year-old family tree traced the descent of the English monarchs back to Adam and Eve, affirming the ancient doctrine that the rule of kings was the will of God.

Created about 1465, this elaborate manuscript runs for almost 30 feet, up and down both sides of a 15 foot roll of parchment. It is illuminated with portraits of Biblical figures as well as English monarchs of both history and myth.

King John, forced to sign Magna Carta at Runnymede.

Magna Carta

Magna Carta—Latin for the "Great Charter"—is the almost 800-year-old English compact which has been revered by generations of the British and American people as the cornerstone of their long tradition of individual liberties.

Magna Carta's enduring fame reflects the dramatic circumstances of its creation. Although it takes the form of a royal charter common at the time—a grant freely bestowed by a willing king upon the subjects whose obedience he enjoyed—the story of Magna Carta's making is very different. It is the story of a kingdom under threat of civil war and a king who had become a tyrant.

King John reigned in England from 1167 to 1216. He raised taxes and increased the services he demanded of his barons. He meddled in the affairs of the Church and squeezed the merchants for money. He appointed dishonest men to govern and waged an unsuccessful war against France. Discontent reached its peak in May of 1215 when the barons formally renounced their feudal allegiance to the King. Without the strength to crush the rebels, King John had no choice but to give in to their demands. At a meadow called Runnymede, he acknowledged defeat by placing his Great Seal to Magna Carta. "Know that," the preamble read, "we have granted also to all free men of our kingdom for us and heirs forever, all the liberties written below, to be had and holden by themselves and their heirs from us and our heirs."

Only a few of the provisions of Magna Carta's text—listed in 63 brief "chapters" or articles—concern what we would understand as civil liberties. Designed to settle differences between King John and his rebellious barons, the chapters cover such issues as the inheritance of lands and titles and the release of hostages. Other chapters concern the royal control of the English forests, rules for fishing in the River Thames, the people's obligations to build bridges, and the ancient duty of the nobles to bear arms for the king.

But Magna Carta is much more than the list of its chapters. The great significance of the Great Charter is that it offers one of the earliest instances in the Anglo-American tradition of the ideal of government based on law—a rule of law rather than a law of rulers.

Winston Churchill wrote of Magna Carta that *Here is a law above the King and which even he must not break. This reaffirmation of a supreme law and its expression in a general charter is the great work of Magna Carta; and this alone justifies the respect in which men have held it . . . . The underlying idea of the sovereignty of law . . . was raised by [Magna Carta] into a doctrine for the national State. And when in subsequent ages the State, swollen with its own authority, has attempted to ride roughshod over the rights or liberties of the subject, it is to this doctrine that appeal has again and again been made, and never, as yet, without success.*

There are a handful of Magna Carta's provisions that bear importantly on the development of the civil liberties in Britain, and later in the American colonies. Chapters 39 and 40 are particularly significant. Chapter 39 reads: "No free man shall be taken or imprisoned or dispossessed, or outlawed, or banished, or in any way destroyed . . . except by the lawful judgement of his peers or by the law of the land." Chapter 40 states "To no one will we sell, to none will we deny or delay right or justice." Here is the source for Anglo-American traditions of due process and trial by jury. The two chapters are ancestral to the Fifth and Sixth amendments of the Bill of Rights 575 years later. And like Magna Carta, the U.S. Constitution would be "the supreme law of the land," a charter which could not be overturned by later rulings.

When King John's successor, Henry III, took the throne agreeing to Magna Carta, the Great Charter became a permanent part of the English nation. In the centuries that followed, many other monarchs were to acknowledge the primacy of Magna Carta. It came to be called "the statute called the Great Charter of the Liberties of England." The simple fact that the language of Magna Carta bestowed its benefits on "free men" held enormous significance. So great has been the success of Magna Carta, and so broadly has it been interpreted, that a document written to protect the nobles from the king has been used to protect all citizens from any governmental oppression.

It may be that this generous spirit of interpreting past laws and liberties lies very near the heart of what is best in the Anglo-American constitutional tradition—a willingness to see the intent of past lawmakers in the light of a new time.

John Locke.

John Locke and the Social Contract

The Americans who founded the United States thought a good deal about the state of nature, the place where natural law prevailed. The state of nature was a mythic landscape philosophers had invented to help them think about what was real about the human condition. It was a way of stripping life down to its bare essentials to see which qualities people were born with and which qualities were the product of civilization.

No one was more influential in mapping the features of the state of nature than the British philosopher John Locke (1632-1704). Locke reasoned that all men were born free and equal, their freedom the gift of God. They had enjoyed this liberty and equality in the state of nature which had come before human societies. The most basic of human rights are life, liberty and property—the ability to earn and hold on to possessions. Humans are not equal in all ways: Some surpass their fellows in strength or intelligence, but all are equally entitled to these natural rights.

However, because people were not equal in their strengths, the state of nature was a dangerous and uncertain condition. Long ago, people had created society for their protection. They had agreed to some limits on their freedom and equality in order to promote their safety and to protect their property. This agreement was the social contract.

The social contract theory had revolutionary implications. Governments had been formed by the consent of the governed for their own benefit. Each member had given up some measure of freedom in return for safety. If the people created government voluntarily and for these purposes, it was reasonable to expect that they also had the right to ". . . alter or abolish it, and to institute a new government, laying its foundation on such principles . . . as to them shall seem most likely to effect their safety and happiness . . . ."

Under the social contract, government is a kind of trust. If government broke the agreement it was tyranny. For the governed to abolish a tyrannical government and form a new one was a sacred duty. Thomas Jefferson, who used Locke's ideas so freely in the Declaration of Independence, had a motto that spoke of that duty. "Rebellion to Tyrants," it read, "is Obedience to God."

The Russian people in 1991 destroy symbols of Communist tyranny. In 1917, their for-bearers tore down similar symbols of the czars.

John Locke, "An Essay Concerning Toleration, 1667," autograph manuscript.

John Locke (1632-1704) was one of the most influential of the thinkers who pointed the way to new ideas of government based on the rights of individuals, rather than the powers of rulers.

In this 48-page autograph manuscript, Locke considered the question of religious toleration, a theme to which he returned throughout his life.

Largely the work of jurist and scholar Sir Edward Cooke, the Petition of Rights was the first of the important British constitutional documents since Magna Carta. It has been called "the second Great Charter of the Liberties of England." A short text of 11 articles, it catalogs Charles' abuses, cites the relevant chapters from Magna Carta and statutes from Edward III's reign forbidding such actions, and concludes by asking that the King now acknowledge his errors and promise not to repeat them. In addition to affirming the principle of parliamentary consent to taxation, the Petition explicitly extended the right of *habeas corpus* and due process of the law to all citizens. It also gave protection from quartering of soldiers in private homes and against the trial of civilians by military courts.

When the Petition was presented to him in 1628, King Charles had no choice but to promise to comply with the document's terms. But the next year, in another fight over money with the House of Commons, the King angrily dismissed Parliament again. For the next 11 years King Charles ruled without a Parliament in open defiance of several of the articles he had promised to obey.

Meanwhile, renewed religious conflict was taking England to the brink of civil war. The King, suspected of sympathies towards the Catholic Church, worked against the Calvinists and other dissenting protestants. A new war threatened, this one with Scotland. Without the means to levy most taxes, the kingdom's financial situation became increasingly perilous. In 1640, the King was compelled to summon a Parliament to London.

Charles fared even worse with the new Parliament, dominated as it was by Puritans and other enemies of the Crown. Actual war between the armies of King Charles and parliamentarians broke out in 1642. Soon all of England was swept up in the fighting. The war continued until 1649, when Charles was captured, tried and beheaded.

The Puritan general Oliver Cromwell eventually assumed the role of head of state as Protector. For more than 10 years, England was without a king, an altogether revolutionary circumstance in 17th-century Europe.

In 1660, weary of 20 years of unrest, the British gladly invited the Stuarts back. Pleasure-loving Charles II took his executed father's place on the throne. Charles' rule was unmarred by statesmanship or civic virtue, but he managed to reign for a full quarter century until his death in 1685.

His place was taken by his brother, James II, last of England's Stuart monarchs. Charles II is thought to have secretly converted to Catholicism before his death, but his brother James went further in openly favoring the Church of Rome. This, along with his attempts to thwart the constitution and his political blunders, caused him to lose the throne after only 3 years. In what would become known as the Glorious Revolution, powerful men in England asked William Prince of Orange, a Dutch protestant grandson of Charles I, to climb onto the throne. William landed in England late in 1688 and James II fled England, never to return.

In January of 1689, Britain entered a new era. A hastily-convened Parliament met in London and proclaimed William and his wife Mary joint sovereigns. By the end of the year 1689, the triumph of Parliament was completed when it passed the Bill of Rights.

The Bill of Rights set out the terms under which Parliament would *permit* William and Mary and all future monarchs to reign in England. Sitting on the English throne had become a statutory, not a hereditary privilege, one which Parliament could revoke or change. The ancient notion of the divine right of kings had been banished forever from the realm.

The Bill of Rights began with a list of the abuses of King James. (In 1776, the Declaration of Independence would offer the world a similar list of misdeeds of another king, the unfortunate George III.)

Non est potestas Super Terram quæ Comparetur ei Iob. 41. 24.

LEVIATHAN
Or
THE MATTER, FORME
and POWER of A COMMON-
WEALTH ECCLESIASTICALL
and CIVIL

By THOMAS HOBBES
of MALMESBVRY.

London
Printed for Andrew Crooke
1651

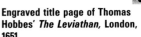

Modern Britons protest the poll tax.

Engraved title page of Thomas Hobbes' *The Leviathan,* London, 1651.

In this clever depiction of the social contract, countless tiny citizens join together to form the gigantic monarch who symbolizes the nation.

The theory of natural rights and the social contract were essential philosophical starting points of the revolution for individual liberties which found expression in the American Bill of Rights.

The problem that remained was how to curb the giant's power.

Thomas Paine.

James II's offenses included many of the old parliamentary complaints: taxation without the consent of Parliament; keeping a standing army in time of peace; and disarming the people. They also included imposing cruel and unusual punishments and excessive bail and fines; and denial of due process. All of these acts, the text continues, *are utterly and directly contrary to the known laws and statutes, and freedom of this realm.*

After recounting King James' abuses, the Bill of Rights declared 13 specific rights of the people. These included:

• Protection from taxation without the consent of the people's representatives. This would become one of the principal causes of the American Revolution.

• The right to petition the government — guaranteed to Americans in the First Amendment.

• The outlawing of standing armies in time of peace — British military occupation of the colonies was another cause of the Revolution.

• The right to bear arms — reflected in the Second Amendment of the U.S. Constitution.

• Protection from excessive bail and cruel and unusual punishments — as in our Eighth Amendment.

And some of the rights named in the Bill of Rights of 1689 are guaranteed to Americans in the body of the Constitution itself.

But however glorious the Revolution of 1689 may have seemed at the time, the rights of British citizens fell far short of those later granted by the American model. In fact, the English Bill of Rights failed to provide many of the freedoms that already existed in the American colonies in the late 17th century. In 1791 Thomas Paine would charge in *The Rights of Man* that the British Bill of

18th century British Parliament in session.

Rights was a mere bargain between the branches of the government to divide up political power at the peoples' expense. In June of 1789, Congressman James Madison, introducing in the U.S. House of Representatives the Bill of Rights amendments to the new Constitution, noted that "[t]he freedom of the press and rights of conscience, those choicest privileges of the people, are unguarded in the British Constitution." Madison knew what he was talking about. Of the five bedrock freedoms in the First Amendment of the U.S. Bill of Rights — of religion, speech, press, assembly and petition — the English people were given only the right to petition their government.

During the 60 years of the struggle between King and Parliament, the English colonists across the ocean were winning footholds all along the American seaboard. The colonies had been few, small and feeble when Charles I came to the throne in 1625. By the time of the Bill of Rights in 1689, they had become strong and populous and thoroughly British provinces. Most of the colonists gloried in the victory of law over arbitrary power. The events in England had put to rest forever the danger of royal absolutism and had established what Britons everywhere knew was surely the most free and enlightened government on earth.

MAD TOM.
or the MAN of RIGHTS.

By the time of the English Bill of Rights in 1689, British colonists were living in settlements up and down the Atlantic coast of North America. Although it included such documents as Magna Carta and the Bill of Rights, the British Constitution had remained for the most part unwritten. The American experience was very different. Some of the colonies had been founded on religious belief, some as a mark of royal favor, some as investments calculated to enrich men back in London. Endeavors like these usually required some sort of written agreement defining the purposes of the venture, the rights and duties of the colonists and of those who would govern them. Americans grew accustomed to thinking of government in such terms. Indeed, the impulse to get the fundamentals of government down in writing came to distinguish the political vision of the English-speaking people of the colonies long before they thought to call themselves Americans.

The first permanent English colony in America, at Jamestown in 1607, set the pattern. The colony's charter — the First Charter of Virginia — was granted by King James I in 1606, before the colonists set sail for the New World. It is the first of the American documents in the long line that runs directly to the U.S. Bill of Rights. The First Charter's most notable assertion is that the colonists,

> . . . in that part of America, commonly called Virginia . . . . all and every the Persons . . . and every of their children . . . shall have and enjoy all Liberties, Franchises, and Immunities . . . to all Intents and Purposes, as if they had been abiding and born, within this our Realm of England . . . .

As the English established new colonies, they tended to claim the same rights as freeborn British subjects, in much the same language. Nowhere were those rights very much enlarged upon; the rights were not closely defined, nor were the ways of securing them often spelled out. And as grants, the charters did not have the force of fundamental law; they could be changed or withdrawn by the

Virginia Laws John Smith, *The Generall History of Virginia, New-England, and the Summer Isles* . . . **By Captain John Smith . . . London, 1624.**

In 1607, a company of adventurers that included John Smith founded the first permanent English colony in America at Jamestown in Virginia. The Virginia colony's royal charter is the first of American documents in the long line that runs directly to the Bill of Rights almost 200 years later. It promised the colonists that

. . . in that part of America, commonly called Virginia . . . . all and every the Persons . . . and every of their children . . . shall have and enjoy all Liberties, Franchises, and Immunities . . . to all Intents and Purposes, as if they had been abiding and born, within this our Realm of England . . .

This copy of Captain Smith's Generall History of Virginia contains a rare autograph letter of the author, soldier and explorer.

grantor. Yet the Americans seemed not to see it that way. They never forgot the promise of their first charters, which they regarded as fundamental law. Those documents became in a sense the Americans' Magna Carta. John Adams would argue many years later that the First Charter of Virginia was "more like a treaty between independent sovereigns than like a charter or grant of privileges from a sovereign to his subjects."

The rights the colonists believed they were entitled to as freeborn Britons included the familiar if rather vague list from Magna Carta and English common law — the right to due process by the law of the land, to fair trial by jury and to the writ of *habeas corpus,* as well as protection from cruel and unusual punishments. They also seemed to think that they had a right to a voice in their government. Assemblies representing some of the people were not long in appearing in most of the colonies.

Of course, the English had not come to America to extend the sway of Magna Carta or find new soil where new constitutional systems could flourish. Jamestown was frankly a money-making venture; it was to a company of investors the King gave the First Charter. The English were also drawn to America for greater glory of their proud island, by the lure of empire, and as another battle in their long and bitter war against the power of Spain and the Catholic Church. They came also to provide an outlet for the landless poor of England. Perhaps most important of all, many came to practice their religions, and sometimes even to allow other people to practice theirs.

The first English settlers to reach Massachusetts — the Pilgrims who landed at Plymouth in 1620 — came to escape the control of a government-established church whose doctrines they did not share. Before going ashore the company drew up the famous Mayflower Compact. Named for the little ship that had carried them safely across the Atlantic, it was the Pilgrims' simple agreement to

. . . combine ourselves together into a civil body politic . . . and by virtue hereof to enact, constitute, and frame such just and equal laws, ordinances, acts, constitutions, and offices . . . for the general good of the colony, unto which we promise all due submission and obedience.

The Compact's 200-word text gave substance to the ideals of participatory democracy and the people's right to agree to the government under which they live. It took as one example the Puritan model of governing a church. Members of the congregation had a vote in electing officers and each congregation was independent and self-governing. This model proved well-suited to managing a colony separated from the mother country by thousands of miles of ocean and weeks of hard sailing. Although Plymouth was eventually absorbed into the larger Massachusetts Bay Colony, the Mayflower Compact lives on as one of the first charters of American liberty. This inclination towards self-government and the conviction that fundamental law should be ordered in written instruments found expression in many later colonial charters.

In 1632 Maryland was chartered as the first proprietary colony when King Charles gave a huge tract of well-watered wilderness to Cecil Calvert, Lord Baltimore.

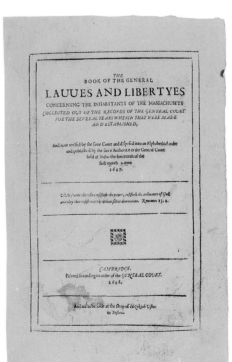

Massachusetts Laws: *The Book of the General Lawes and Libertyes Concerning the Inhabitants of Massachusets....,* **Cambridge, 1648.**

This surpassingly rare volume is the only surviving copy of the printing of an early Massachusetts legal code. To restrain the colony's governing officers, the people of Massachusetts Bay demanded a written code of laws. The result was first published in this book, the earliest surviving collection of laws printed in British America.

Among the *"Libertyes"* the code affirmed were the right to trial by jury (Sixth Amendment of the Bill of Rights); and protection from double jeopardy, forced confessions and cruel and unusual punishments (Fifth and Eighth amendments).

From the beginning Maryland offered broad religious toleration and representative government was soon established in the colony. Although it was a royal grant to a single man, and so a sort of monarchy in miniature, the Charter of Maryland contained a famous clause which allowed for a measure of representative government. The laws made by the Lord Proprietor, it declared, were to be approved by the *"Free-Men of the same Province, or the greater Part of them, or their Delegates or Deputies . . . ."*

In 1639 the colony's popular government took steps to safeguard individual liberties when the Maryland Assembly passed the "Act for the liberties of the people," giving citizens "all such rights liberties immunities privileges and free customs . . . as any natural born subject of England hath . . . ." The Act specifically guaranteed due process of law, in much the same language as Chapter 39 of Magna Carta.

Probably the earliest of American bills of rights is to be found in the Massachusetts Body of Liberties of 1641. One of the most important and influential of colonial constitutional documents, this code grew out of the people's desire for a written source for the colony's laws and for limits on the powers of the magistrates, the governing officers of Massachusetts Bay. It was the creation of the people of Massachusetts Bay, rather than a charter issued by a distant king or proprietor. Those who drafted the Body of Liberties had said they meant to frame it "in resemblance to a Magna Carta." Although its provisions are posed as recommendations to the magistrates, rather than laws binding them, it was in many respects a bold and sweeping call for individual rights. The Body of Liberties recommended a measure of religious toleration; due process by the law of the land; trial by jury and the right to counsel; freedom of speech in the courts and colonial assemblies. It also offered protection against cruel and unusual punishments and second trials for the same offense. All of these rights were later safeguarded in the federal Bill of Rights.

America has been blessed by a rich diversity of religious faiths.

Built in the year 1683. Taken down 175
45 feet by 40 – 16 in the walls. Seat
20 feet to an inch. It stood where
the first Church now stands.

MEETING HOUSE

24

Roger Williams.

Roger Williams
"Lively Experiment"

Roger Williams was born in London about 1603 and died in 1683 in Rhode Island, the American colony he founded. He had come to Massachusetts as a young man in 1631. Not finding there a community lighted by his own vision of religious freedom, brotherhood and justice, Williams proceeded to create that community himself.

He landed in the Puritan colony of Massachusetts-Bay and got into trouble almost at once. The Puritans recognized him as "a godly man" and offered him a congregation of his own. But Williams believed the Puritans had not separated themselves enough from the Church of England and didn't hesitate to say so, repeatedly. He also decried the Puritans' enforcement of their brand of orthodoxy— "forced worship is false worship"—he said. These "newe & dangerous opinions" made Williams an enemy of the Puritan church-state. He was given a chance to hold his tongue and when he refused, he was banished from Massachusetts for life.

In 1636 Williams set off into the wilderness with a few followers in the dead of winter. He went south, built a log cabin and called it Providence. He had founded Rhode Island and Providence Plantations. From the very start, the new settlement offered inhabitants a greater degree of religious freedom than they were likely to find anywhere else on earth. This, in the words of the 1663 Charter of Rhode Island, was Roger Williams' "lively experiment:"

> ... That it is much on their hearts (if they may be permitted), to hold forth a livlie experiment, that a most flourishing civill state may stand and best bee maintained ... with a full liberties in religious concernements ....

Rhode Island's charter was the first instance of religious freedom's incorporation into fundamental law in America. In Rhode Island, religious freedom was not just an act of legislation or grant of a proprietor.

In 1644 Williams published his best known work, *THE BLOUDY TENENT OF PERSECUTION, for the cause of CONSCIENCE.* Here he wrote with compelling simplicity of the tragic irony of Christians slaughtering each other in the name of the Prince of Peace and argued that,

> God requireth not an uniformity of Religion to be enacted and inforced in any civill state; which inforced uniformity (sooner or later) is the greatest occasion of civill Warre ....

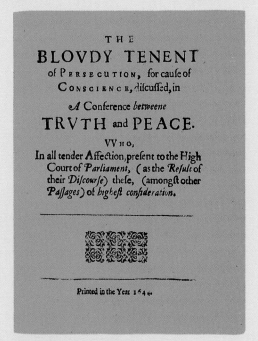

THE
BLOVDY TENENT,
of PERSECUTION, for caufe of
CONSCIENCE, difcuffed, in

A Conference betweene
TRVTH and PEACE.

VVHO,
In all tender Affection, prefent to the High
Court of *Parliament,* (as the *Refult* of
their *Difcourfe*) thefe, (amongft other
Paffages) of *higheft confideration.*

Printed in the Year 1644.

Roger Williams, *the Bloudy Tenent of Persecution, for the cause of Conscience,* . . . London, 1644.

In the *Bloudy Tenent,* Williams argued that the carnage of Europe's unending religious warfare was not a fit offering to "Jesus Christ the Prince of Peace."

In Biblical imagery, Williams wrote that there should be "a wall of separation between the garden of the Church and the wilderness of the world . . . ." Such a separation became the supreme law of a new nation with the first words of the U.S. Bill of Rights—

"Congress Shall make no law respecting an establishment of religion, or prohibiting the free exercise thereof . . . ."

Most advocates of religious toleration stopped short of extending protection to non-Christian faiths. But, in *The Bloudy Tenent of Persecution,* Williams asserted that

> It is the will and command of God, that . . . a permission of the most Paganish, Jewish, Turkish or Antichristian consciences and worships bee granted to all men in all Nations . . . they are to bee fought against with . . . the Sword of God's Spirit, the Word of God . . . .

Roger Williams joined his dedication to religious freedom with a belief in popular government, declaring that *"the Soveraigne, originall, and foundation of civill power lies in the people . . . ."* and that *"Kings or Parliaments,* [or] *States . . ."* could legitimately possess only the power given them by the people, and *"that a People may erect and establish what forme of Government seemes to them* [best] *. . . ."*

Williams' was that distinctly American vision of the new nation as a shining city. Williams saw civil and religious freedom, supported by liberty and equality for all, as mutually supporting and mutually revealed as God's will—the twin pillars of the new Jerusalem. Expressing his conviction in appropriately Biblical imagery, Williams had written that there should be "a wall of separation between the garden of the Church and the wilderness of the world . . . ."

One hundred and fifty years later, President Thomas Jefferson echoed Williams when he said that the purpose of the first clause of the First Amendment—*Congress shall make no law respecting an establishment of religion, or prohibiting the free exercise thereof . . .*—was to build a "wall of separation between church and state . . . ."

Roger Williams sought peaceful relations with Native Americans.

Religious practices unknown to Colonial America, here a Buddhist monk at prayer, have generally found toleration under our Bill of Rights.

The Charter of Rhode Island and Providence Plantations in 1663, (discussed in the accompanying profile of Roger Williams), gave inhabitants very nearly complete freedom of religion. In this regard Rhode Island was probably the most enlightened place on earth. The Rhode Island Charter shaped the provisions for religious toleration in many subsequent colonial charters, including those of Pennsylvania, Carolina and New Jersey.

Pennsylvania was a proprietary colony with a twist — the proprietor himself was a member of a persecuted sect. As a young man William Penn had done time in jail in both England and Ireland for his Quaker beliefs. But now he was the sole proprietor (thanks to a timely loan of £18,000 his father had made to the exiled Charles II before the Restoration) of an immense chunk of America. Penn proposed to manage it as a "Holy Experiment," a phrase he may well have borrowed from Roger Williams' 1663 Rhode Island Charter. Penn gave form to his beliefs in sketching the outlines of a society with energetic representative government, protection of basic civil liberties and a large measure of religious toleration. The rights of the colonists were later enlarged upon in the Pennsylvania Charter of Privileges in 1701.

As a new century began in 1701, the pattern was largely fixed. While the colonies would continue to grow in population and wealth, the basic political structures were in place. Most important in the colonial experience had been the Americans' claim to the rights of English subjects, the growth of representative government and the remarkable degree of religious freedom enjoyed in many colonies.

Also notable was the way in which the colonies tended to borrow and copy from each other's charters, laws and constitutions. This practice of cross-fertilization made it easy for the colonies to agree on the meaning of liberty when conflict with Britain came in the 1760s.

During the first half of the 18th century, the colonies matured in relative isolation; the British were preoccupied with other matters. Many colonies exercised almost complete self-government; they were comfortable with the blessings of liberty and had come to consider them theirs by right.

The second half of the century was very different. In 1759, the British found themselves embroiled in a great war of empire against France. The trans-Atlantic conflict of the Seven Years War — called the French and Indian War by the Americans — changed the old balance of the British empire.

Images of Williamsburg, the capital of Colonial Virginia.

27

THE CASE OF JOHN PETER ZENGER

Like some 20th-century reporter going to jail for defying a court order to reveal his sources, John Peter Zenger (1697-1746) spent nearly a year behind bars waiting to be tried on printing newspaper stories attacking the royal governor of New York. In 1735 he finally went to trial for publishing "seditious slanders." It proved to be one of the most famous cases in colonial history, closely studied in both England and America.

Freedom of the press was not one of the "rights of freeborn Englishmen" that the colonists carried with them to America. A system of censorship, the "licensing" of books, had been introduced by Henry VIII in 1538. Heretical and seditious works were outlawed under the licensing system. In America, as early as 1660, a Virginian had been sentenced for criticizing the colony's legislative assembly. And even the Quaker William Penn drew the line at a free press in Pennsylvania.

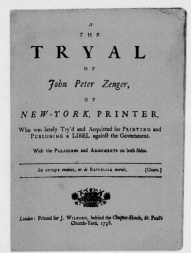

Today, the dictionary tells us that libel is "any false written statement" against an individual. But it was defined differently by the English common law of Zenger's day. Then criminal libel was the publication of charges against any public official, or against the laws of the state, or any institution established by those laws. The truth of the charges was not the issue. Indeed the greater the truth, the greater and more to be condemned was the libel.

Zenger printed the colony's opposition newspaper, set up by a group of citizens determined to resist the policies of the new royal governor, William Cosby. Cosby was a man who can fairly be described as crooked, greedy and arrogant. Those who wrote the attacks on the governor were cautious or cowardly enough not to sign their names to the offending pieces and so it was the paper's publisher, Peter Zenger, who was charged.

At the trial Zenger was brilliantly defended by Andrew Hamilton of Philadelphia. The common law prescribed that the task of a jury in a criminal libel case was to decide only if the accused had in fact made the statements specified in the charges. If so, the determination of whether those statements were actually libelous would be made by the judge, who would also pass sentence.

However, Andrew Hamilton's defense flew in the face of the ancient custom. He freely admitted that his client had made the statements. He appealed to the court to allow the accuracy of the newspaper's accusations against Governor Cosby to be considered as evidence. When the court denied the motion, Hamilton made the same appeal to the jury, which was considerably more obliging. They promptly returned a verdict of not guilty. Those 12 men understood that William Cosby was a *public* official, not a slandered private citizen, and that the accusations against him not only concerned public business, but were largely true.

The verdict was greeted with jubilation throughout America and a published account circulated widely on both sides of the Atlantic. Zenger's acquittal changed no laws; it did serve to strengthen the people's freedom to challenge the conduct of public men in the public press.

Daniel Ellsberg, who leaked the *Pentagon Papers* to the *New York Times,* and a political cartoon of Richard Nixon, demonstrate that debates about the meaning of a free press are still very much with us.

NIXON'S REVENGE

CHAPTER

3

The American Crisis: ROAD TO REVOLUTION

In 1763, 150 years after the English founded their first colony in North America, an English victory in the French and Indian War gave them control of most of the continent. It was a great triumph for the British—those who lived in Britain and those who lived in Britain's American colonies.

Or so it seemed. In just 12 years, from the victory of 1763 to the firing of the first shots of the Revolution at Lexington and Concord in 1775, the British and the colonists were propelled into a future few of them would have thought possible. A string of crises led them on a steady march to rebellion and war, separation and independence. The swift course of the building conflict can be traced through a series of laws passed by the British government followed by the American reaction. It makes for a chronicle of misunderstanding compounded by monumental political ineptitude.

Britain's victory over the French had been expensive as well as glorious—in 1763 the country's national debt had swollen to £125 million. Moreover, when France gave up its American territories, Britain gained an enormous new area to defend and garrison. The government would need all the revenue it could get and taxing the American colonies seemed to be one reasonable source. It was thought in London that the Americans had benefited more from the war and that they could well afford to contribute towards the cost. The burden of taxation already fell less heavily on the colonists. The British position on these matters had considerable merit. The ministers in London forgot, however, that many colonists believed in the principle that to be taxed, the colonists should be represented in Parliament. It was to prove a fatal miscalculation.

The British set about to raise money in the colonies through acts of Parliament setting fees or levying taxes against various imports. The most famous of them is the Stamp Act of 1765 that taxed many uses of paper, everything from executing a deed to buying a newspaper. These attempts to tax the colonies were double failures. Not only did Parliament's taxes fail to raise money, they also infuriated the Americans.

At about the same time, Britain also decided to station large permanent Army garrisons in America, the first such instance in peacetime. The Foreign Office forgot that here, too, they were violating one of the fundamental principles of the British Constitution. A standing army in time of peace had been condemned in the British Bill of Rights in 1689.

Finally, a new king, George III, had taken the throne in 1761. George III was more bad luck for the British; he was an obtuse and stubborn man whose presence on the throne made it easier for the Americans to renounce their ancient loyalties to the Crown.

The first official American response to the Stamp Act came from the Virginia House of Burgesses, which declared that "... the Taxation of a People by themselves, or by Persons chosen by themselves to represent them ... is ... the distinguishing characteristic of British Freedom, without which the ancient Constitution cannot exist ...." Even more alarming than taxes to the Americans were several other provisions of the Stamp Act. In order to enforce collection and curb smuggling, government agents were authorized to search for untaxed goods without specific warrants. Accused Americans could be taken to Britain for trial by an admiralty court. The colonists viewed these measures as violations of the rights of Englishmen, some dating back to Magna Carta—the right to trial by a jury of one's peers, in the locality where the offense was alleged to have taken place; and the right to due process by the law of the land. "[I]t is directly repugnant to the Great Charter itself," John Adams said.

In an unusual display of colonial unity, nine colonies sent delegates to a Stamp Act Congress, which resolved that taxation without representation threatened their most sacred rights: ". . . such Power has a manifest Tendency to destroy British as well as American Freedom."

The Stamp Act Congress further stated that Americans had no duty to obey the Act, and obey they did not. They responded with boycotts of British goods and nonimportation associations; they smuggled goods to avoid paying duties; they formed committees of correspondence, assemblies and congresses. Since theirs was at first a struggle for their legal rights, carried out by legal means, the colonists also drafted petitions, wrote letters, and debated the issues of the day in newspapers and pamphlets.

Resistance also took more violent forms. Popular anger focused on the most obvious targets—the tax collectors themselves. Throughout the colonies they were hounded out of office, subjected to tarring and feathering, systematically frightened into resigning. In the end, American opposition nullified the Stamp Act; unenforceable, it was repealed in 1766.

Having caved in on the Stamp Act, Parliament felt compelled at least to declare its constitutional authority to rule over the colonies. This they did in the Declaratory Act of 1766, which had the effect of inflaming American tempers all the more. In 1767 the crisis was ratchetted up another notch when Parliament tried again to tax the colonies and to govern them through a series of measures called the Townshend Acts. The Townshend Acts levied taxes on imports of lead, paint, paper, glass and, most famously, on tea, at a rate of 3 pence per pound.

Even more tyrannical in American eyes were the provisions regarding enforcement of the acts and the quartering of British troops in New York and Boston. Boston was a port built on trade, as well as a hotbed of patriot resistance, and it was here that opposition to the import duties was the most violent. To cow the Bostonians into submission, the British sent troops to occupy the city in 1768.

The "Sons of Liberty" register their dissatisfaction with British taxes and British tax collectors while other patriots turn Boston harbor into the world's biggest teapot.

Although the patriots are depicted as thugs in this English cartoon, American resistance was grounded on ancient principles of the British Constitution.

"The Bostonians Paying the Excise-Man or Tarring & Feathering," 1830 printing of 1774 mezzotint attributed to Philip Dawe, London.

EXTRACTS

FROM THE

VOTES and PROCEEDINGS

Of the AMERICAN CONTINENTAL

CONGRESS,

Held at PHILADELPHIA on the
5th of *September* 1774.

CONTAINING

The BILL of RIGHTS, a Lift of GRIEVANCES, Occafional Refolves, the *Affociation*, an *Addrefs* to the PEOPLE of GREAT-BRITAIN, and a *Memorial* to the INHABITANTS of the BRITISH AMERICAN COLONIES.

Publifhed by order of the CONGRESS.

PHILADELPHIA:
Printed by WILLIAM and THOMAS BRADFORD,
October 27th, M,DCC,LXXIV.

Extracts from the Proceedings of the American Continental Congress, held at Philadelphia, September 5, 1774. Containing the Bill of Rights, . . . Philadelphia, [1774].

Forced to the brink of rebellion by Britain's heavy-handed efforts to tax the colonies, the First Continental Congress affirmed the rights Americans would soon be fighting to protect.

In 1774 the Continental Congress' "Bill of Rights" proclaimed Americans' rights to life, liberty, and property; to be taxed only by their own representatives; to trial by jury in their own neighborhood; and to protection from unreasonable searches and seizures and from military occupation in time of peace.

The BLOODY MASSACRE perpetrated in King—t.Street BOSTON on Mar.h5.1770 by a party of the 29.th REG.T

BUTCHER'S HALL

CUSTOMHOUSE

Engrav'd Printed & Sold by PAUL REVERE BOSTON

ppy BOSTON! fee thy Sons deplore,
hallow'd Walks befmear'd with guiltlefs Gore:
e faithlefs P—n and his favage Bands,
murd'rous Rancour ftretch their bloody Hands;
fierce Barbarians grinning o'er their Prey,
rove the Carnage, and enjoy the Day.

If fcalding drops from Rage from Anguifh Wrung
If fpeechlefs Sorrows lab'ring for a Tongue,
Or if a weeping World can ought appeafe
The plaintive Ghofts of Victims fuch as thefe;
The Patriot's copious Tears for each are fhed,
A glorious Tribute which embalms the Dead.

But know, FATE fummons to that awful Goal,
Where JUSTICE ftrips the Murd'rer of his Soul
Should venal C—ts the fcandal of the Land,
Snatch the relentlefs Villain from her Hand,
Keen Execrations on this Plate infcrib'd,
Shall reach a JUDGE who never can be brib'd.

he unhappy Sufferers were Meff.rs SAM.L GRAY, SAM.L MAVERICK, JAM.S CALDWELL, CRISPUS ATTUCKS & PAT.K CAR
Killed. Six wounded two of them (CHRIST.R MONK & JOHN CLARK) Mortally

The Boston Massacre inflamed patriot emotions against the British Governments' use of force. The shootings of students at Kent State in 1970 raised similar passion in a new generation.

Paul Revere, "The Bloody Massacre perpetrated in . . . Boston on March 5th 1770 . . . ." Hand-colored engraving, Boston, 1770.

The crash of British muskets fired into a riotous Boston crowd foretold the American Revolution's 8 years of bloody warfare.

The Bill of Rights' Second and Third amendments, which forbid the quartering of troops and protect the right to bear arms, are evidence of how much Americans resented military occupation.

This rare engraving of the "Bloody Massacre" was executed by Paul Revere, the famous Boston silversmith and patriot leader.

George III, King of Great Britain and Ireland, et cetera, to [Thomas] Townshend, 19 November 1782, autograph letter signed with initials.

America's last king bows to what had become the inevitable at Yorktown a year before and instructs his foreign minister to go ahead with the treaty in which Britain must acknowledge the independence of her 13 former colonies.

It is hardly surprising that King George, the man Jefferson had reviled as tyrant in the Declaration of Independence, would be among the last to agree to the Declaration's central proposition . . . "that these United Colonies are FREE and INDEPENDENT STATES."

Even at this late hour, King George had trouble stomaching the word independence, and changed it to separation, which he misspelled.

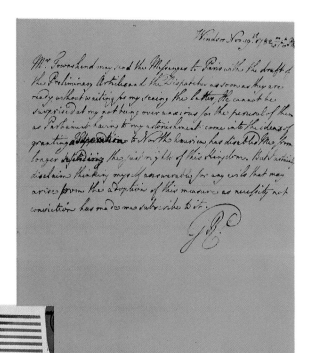

The resignation of President Nixon, the only president to do so, demonstrated how a leader can fall in our constitutional system.

"The Horse America, Throwing his Master,"
London, 1779, hand-colored engraving. (Detail)

The soldiers were a source of unending rancor. Conflict between the citizens and the soldiers culminated in the notorious "Boston Massacre" in 1770. Shots had been fired and the two sides moved closer to civil war.

The Townshend taxes also soon proved unenforceable failures and most were repealed in 1770. The one remaining import duty—on tea—was not much more acceptable to the Bostonians than the many former taxes. In late 1773 a band of patriots disguised as Indians turned Boston harbor into the world's biggest teapot.

In retaliation for the Boston Tea Party, the British passed in 1774 the measures that Americans immediately dubbed the "Intolerable Acts." Harshest of all was the Boston Port Act, which closed the city's harbor to nearly all trade. The Massachusetts Government Act sought to strengthen Parliament's hand by actually changing the colony's royal charter, something that had never been done before. A new quartering act declared that British troops could be housed in private homes.

The British had made another grave mistake. They had hoped to isolate Massachusetts and restore peace to the colonies, but instead the Intolerable Acts further united the colonists against them. The Americans' response was the calling of the First Continental Congress of 1774.

The Continental Congress was the direct ancestor of the government of the United States, and it would remain the closest thing to a central government the Americans would have until the beginnings of the first federal administration in 1789. Twelve of the 13 colonies sent delegates to the Congress. They included men like John Adams and Sam Adams from Massachusetts, and George Washington and Patrick Henry from Virginia. Present in spirit if not in flesh was Thomas Jefferson whose influential pamphlet *Summary View of the Rights of British America* (1774) had anticipated many of the positions to be adopted by the Congress. Meeting in Philadelphia in the fall of 1774, the Continental Congress moved boldly to declare the rights Americans

THOMAS JEFFERSON
1743-1826

Thomas Jefferson.

Thomas Jefferson's entry in one biographical dictionary describes him as "statesman, diplomat, author, scientist, architect, apostle of freedom and enlightenment." To these titles one might add historian, lawyer, agronomist, librarian and archivist, musician, philosopher and member of learned societies, inventor, horticulturalist, linguist, et cetera. Jefferson himself, however, gave very specific instructions— "not a word more," he charged— regarding the several facts he wished recorded on his gravestone at Monticello:

Here was buried

Thomas Jefferson

Author of the Declaration of American Independence

of the Statute of Virginia for religious freedom

& Father of the University of Virginia

Mr. Jefferson did not care to mention his services as President of the United States, as Vice President, as Washington's first Secretary of State, as governor of Virginia, delegate to the Virginia House of Burgesses and the Continental Congress or American ambassador to France. Jefferson also had a part to play in the creation of the Bill of Rights.

In July 1774 Thomas Jefferson was too sick to make the trip from his home to the Virginia convention meeting in Williamsburg to plan the colony's response to the crisis set off by the Intolerable Acts' closing of Boston harbor. But the young lawyer had already drafted a set of resolutions that he sent to the convention in his place, with the idea that they might serve as instructions for the Virginia delegation headed for the Continental Congress in Philadelphia. Soon published as a pamphlet,

Jefferson's *A Summary View of the Rights of British America . . .* (Williamsburg, 1774), was framed as an address to King George. Although it retained some of the old-fashioned tone of deference toward the Crown, the Summary View was studded with hard-edged claims of American rights. In it, the young Virginian pointedly reminded His Royal Highness that kings were "the servants, not the proprietors of the people." Reprinted in Britain and America, the pamphlet won Jefferson "the reputation of a masterly pen." It was in large part because of that reputation that Thomas Jefferson was entrusted with drafting a document that would signify the end of "British America."

Jefferson was 33 years old the summer he wrote the Declaration of Independence. It took him about two weeks to compose, in one of history's most celebrated documents, the classic statement of American rights and revolutionary aspirations. The Declaration of Independence is not an official state paper of the government of the United States, since no such nation then existed. But it has always been justly regarded as the first of the country's great foundation documents.

The second of the deeds Thomas Jefferson wanted chiselled into his tombstone was his authorship of the Statute of Virginia for Religious Freedom. Jefferson served out the Revolutionary War as a delegate to the Continental Congress and as the governor of Virginia. In Virginia he gave his most devoted efforts to molding the ancient colony's constitution and legal code into a form suitable for the new republican state. Close to the heart of Jefferson's republican vision was complete freedom of religion. This meant severing of all ties between the government of Virginia and the long-established Church of England.

In Virginia the most important form of state support for the Church of England was taxation. To overturn the old order, Jefferson drafted a bill, "an Act for establishing Religious Freedom," which after ten years, was finally pushed through the Virginia legislature by James Madison. It was not until 1786 that James Madison could write to Jefferson in France that the passage of the Act had "extinguished forever the ambitious hope of making laws for the human mind." It was an important step towards the protection of religious freedom in the First Amendment of the Bill of Rights.

[Virginia Declaration of Rights]
Ordinances . . . of Virginia . . . 1776,
Williamsburg, [May 1776].

George Mason's Virginia Declaration of Rights was the chief source of the federal Bill of Rights.

As though he had spent his life preparing for the task, Mason dominated the committee appointed to draft a declaration of rights and a state constitution. His *Ordinances...of Virginia* gave Americans a hard-edged vindication of the ideals that had launched their revolution.

FORGING ARMS FOR THE MINUTE-MEN.

The right of citizens to bear arms, which originated as hedge against tyranny during the Revolution, has become subject to modern debate between those supporting and opposing gun control.

ORDINANCES

PASSED AT A GENERAL CONVENTION

OF DELEGATES AND REPRESENTATIVES,

From the several COUNTIES and CORPORATIONS

OF VIRGINIA,

HELD AT THE CAPITOL,

IN THE CITY OF WILLIAMSBURG,

ON MONDAY THE 6th OF MAY,

ANNO DOM: 1776.

WILLIAMSBURG:
PRINTED BY ALEXANDER PURDIE.
PRINTER TO THE COMMONWEALTH.

A N.W. VIEW OF THE STATE HOUSE IN PHILADELPHIA taken 1778

were determined to defend. These they set forth in a "bill of rights," a document printed and reprinted throughout the colonies as *The Declaration and Resolves of the American Continental Congress, Containing the Bill of Rights, a List of Grievances* . . . . This is probably the first time Americans used the term bill of rights to describe their liberties.

The American people were, they declared, "entitled to life, liberty, and property . . ."; "to all the rights, liberties, and immunities of free and natural born [British] subjects . . ."; and "to the great and inestimable privilege of being tried by their peers of the vicinage [vicinity]." They also claimed "a right peaceably to assemble, consider of their grievances, and petition the King." And the Continental Congress raised again in its bill of rights the two key constitutional issues which had played so large a role in provoking the present crisis. They were the people's right to be taxed only by their own representatives and their right to protection from standing armies in time of peace.

The first Continental Congress adjourned at the end of October 1774. Many of the departing delegates must have suspected that a final break with Britain was now inevitable. In fact, only half a year remained until the momentous clash at Lexington and Concord in April 1775. Men died there. Many more died at Bunker Hill two months later. Rather than a fight with a faction of extremists, or with a single rebellious colony, the British had a full scale revolution on their hands. People throughout the colonies considered the Redcoats' volleys in Massachusetts to be an attack on all Americans.

The second Continental Congress, meeting in Philadelphia, moved swiftly to dispatch one of its own members to take command of the patriot army besieging the Redcoats in Boston. Colonel George Washington, the Virginia delegate famous for the part he had played leading his colony's forces in the French and Indian War, had appeared at the Congress in May 1775 wearing his old redcoat militia uniform. His fellow delegates took the hint and named Washington commander-in-chief of the new Continental Army, bumping the colonel all the way up to four-star rank with a flourish of oratory. It was one of the best decisions the Continental Congress would ever make.

The Revolution had been underway for more than a year when the Congress made another good decision and declared *"THAT these United Colonies are, and of right ought to be, FREE and INDEPENDENT STATES."* It took another seven years of fighting, waiting and negotiating before the British were compelled to acknowledge the Declaration of Independence's central proposition. When peace finally came in 1783, Americans would once again turn their attention to the problem of building a government which would secure the rights and liberties for which they had fought.

Students provide aid for demonstrator shot at Kent State.

CHAPTER 4

NEW ORDER OF THE AGES

In 1783, Britain signed the Treaty of Peace conceding with an echo of the Declaration of Independence that her former colonies were at last "free sovereign & independent states." The victorious Americans faced a task as formidable as winning the Revolutionary War. Now they had to fashion a plan for a strong national government while securing the liberties for which the Continental Army had fought.

General Washington's soldiers had waged their war under the Articles of Confederation, drafted by the Continental Congress in 1777 and finally ratified in 1781, the same year Yorktown had clinched American independence. Born of military necessity, the Articles of Confederation was a "firm league of friendship," created by the rebelling colonies "for their common defense, the security of their Liberties, and their mutual and general welfare . . . ." Each state retained "its sovereignty, freedom and independence."

Even in wartime, the Articles of Confederation was a poor basis for effective national government. When victory removed the glue of common peril, the weakness of Congress appeared pitiable. The Articles granted no power to levy taxes, to regulate commerce, to make foreign treaties or to raise an army. The nation's treasury was worse than empty — the government owed great sums it had no way of repaying.

By 1787 the outcome of the American experiment was in doubt. Many Europeans waited in the cheerful expectation that the loose confederation would dissolve into a set of squabbling little seminations. Some said the territory of the United States was too large for any but a despotic government to rule over. Some frankly detested the idea of self-government. Should the Americans fail, it would be, as George Washington predicted, "a triumph for the advocates of despotism."

Convinced that the infant United States could not survive under the Articles, those who favored a stronger central government succeeded in bringing the Constitutional Convention to Philadelphia in May 1787.

While Americans recognized the perils they faced under the Articles of Confederation, there was less concern about the preservation of the individual liberties for which the Revolution had been fought. After all, the rights of the people were safeguarded by the constitutions and declarations of rights of the states themselves. The overriding issue at the Convention of 1787 was not liberty, but power. What powers would the national government have and who would wield those powers? Just a few days after the Convention opened, the delegates began debating the resolutions known as the Virginia Plan. While it sketched the outlines of the strong government the Convention would eventually agree upon, the Virginia Plan also set off conflict by proposing that representation in the national legislature be based on population. This formula was unacceptable to the small states. Throughout the summer the grand assembly of American statesmen argued, maneuvered and compromised. Finally they came up with a plan for a government they could all agree on, one they could hope the constituents at home would accept also. It was a remarkable achievement in spite of the fact that the

The Constitutional Convention.

delegates had swept the issue of slavery under the rug to achieve consensus. This compromise continued the incalculable suffering of millions of black slaves until the bloodshed of the Civil War ended slavery forever.

The delegates had come to Philadelphia to create a powerful national government. By the end of the summer some of them began really to fear that the new government might be strong enough to threaten the people's liberties. Perhaps the state governments would be so over-shadowed that they could no longer be relied on for protection. The Constitution they had drafted was styled "the supreme law of the land"; the new federal government would have power to act directly on the people. Others believed that enumerating the powers of the new government, separating the three branches, and adding checks and balances, would constrain federal power.

George Mason, one of the most influential members of the Convention, and probably its most devoted champion of individual liberties, was not convinced. Mason had declared that the ". . . pole star of my political conduct [is] the preservation of the rights of the people." On September 12, 1787, when the tired delegates could finally look forward to the end of the Convention, the author of the Virginia Declaration of Rights made his famous plea to add a bill of rights to the nearly completed Constitution. James Madison reported that,

> Col: Mason . . . wished the plan had been prefaced with a Bill of Rights & would second a Motion if made for that purpose—It would give great quiet to the people; and with the aid of the State declaration a bill might be prepared in a few hours.

(Many of those state declarations were of course modelled on Mason's Virginia Declaration.) Mason got the motion he asked for. But with the delegations voting as states, the Convention unanimously rejected it. The delegates were ready to go home. But more than weary expediency guided their decision to turn aside the call for a national bill of rights. One delegate probably spoke for most of them when he said that, "The State Declarations of Rights are not repealed by this Constitution; and being in force are sufficient.

"A week after proposing a bill of rights, George Mason and two other delegates refused to join their 39 colleagues in signing the Constitution. Mason angrily claimed "that he would sooner chop off his right hand than put it to the Constitution as it now stands." He called for another convention. The Constitution went to the states; now it was up to them—the document provided that ratification by nine would establish the new government.

George Washington.

THE FEDERALIST DEBATE

"If men were angels, no government would be necessary."
—James Madison, *Federalist* No. 51

The contest to ratify the Constitution was a war of words, fought in the newspapers and in a flurry of tracts and pamphlets. In the pages of *The Federalist*, the Constitution's supporters deployed their biggest guns.

In October 1787, just a month after the Convention sent the Constitution to the states for approval, the bitterly-contested ratification fight was already well underway. Columns attacking the proposed plan of government began appearing in the New York papers. New York was one of the handful of really critical states; if it failed to ratify, the Constitution was probably sunk. Alexander Hamilton organized the Federalist counterattack. Enlisting John Jay and James Madison, Hamilton announced the intention of "Publius" to present a thorough defense of the new Constitution in a series of essays. Theirs has been called the "most famous literary and political partnership in American history," and no less an authority than Thomas Jefferson described *The Federalist* as the "best commentary on the principles of government which ever was written."

In all "Publius" was to submit 85 numbered essays for the consideration of the public. But John Jay ended up writing only 5 of them. Hamilton and Madison carried the project, producing 51 and 29 pieces respectively. The two men turned their essays out at a prodigious rate, in some cases writing them faster than they could be published.

In *Federalist* No. 1, Hamilton set the tone for the series when he declared that

". . . it seems to have been reserved to the people of this country, to decide the important question, whether societies of men are really capable or not, of establishing good government from reflection and choice, or whether they are forever destined to depend, for their political constitutions, on accident and force."

Was the American experiment, in other words, really destined to establish a new order of the ages? The essays that followed examined the weaknesses of the Articles of Confederation, the need for a vigorous national government and the republican ideals and practices which had shaped the drafting of the Constitution.

In No. 84, Alexander Hamilton offered *The Federalist's* most persuasive rebuttal to those who claimed the Constitution's lack of a bill of rights endangered the people's liberties. He began by pointing out that several of the states—6 in all—had themselves no bill of rights and that this lack had caused little concern in the past. He then noted that the Constitution in fact protected a number of specific rights, and so he declared, "the truth is the Constitution is itself in every rational sense, and to every useful purpose, a Bill of Rights." He went on to list those protections. They included the right to habeas corpus and to jury trial in criminal cases. A prohibition of titles of nobility and religious test for office holders, a strict definition of treason, and a guarantee of republican governments in the states were also included.

Here, however, Hamilton had stumbled onto treacherous ground. The Constitution's critics had not overlooked its clauses covering personal freedoms. In fact, they had argued that because these rights were protected, other, unspecified rights were by implication unguarded. This error on the part of the framers had made the Constitution's ratification more difficult and the compromise on a federal bill of rights all the more necessary.

Hamilton then articulated the core Federalist argument—that no bill of rights was needed since the Constitution gave the new government no power to violate individual rights:

"For why declare that things shall not be done which there is no power to do? Why, for instance, should it be said, that liberty of the press shall not be restrained, when no power is given by which restrictions may be imposed?"

In the last essay of the series, *The Federalist* No. 85, Hamilton conceded that a bill of rights could be added to the Constitution, but only after New York had ratified. As in Virginia, there were in New York opponents of the Constitution who insisted on "previous amendment," that is, adding protections of individual liberties before the state ratified. Hamilton countered by arguing that "it will be far more easy to obtain subsequent than previous amendments." In the end the New York ratifying convention did come out for "subsequent amendments." New York ratified in July 1788, the 11th state to do so, and the 5th to ratify with an official recommendation to create a national bill of rights.

Alexander Hamilton.

In leaving out a bill of rights, the Federalists, as the supporters of the new Constitution soon came to be called, had made a major mistake, one that threatened to lose them the struggle for ratification.

Ratification was a hard-fought contest in most of the states. The loose coalition of the Constitution's opponents—who came to be known as Anti-Federalists—had many fears about the new government, but they recognized that their most powerful weapon was the omission of a declaration of rights. They hammered on the theme in one state after another. It was the voice of the people themselves that soon convinced the Federalists that a national bill of rights was indispensable.

The Federalists stuck to their core argument against a bill of rights throughout the ratification debates. The Constitution, they claimed, granted only certain powers to the central government and there was no need to fear the government could or would take more. And since the state declarations of rights remained in force, a federal bill of rights would be unnecessary. As Alexander Hamilton put it in *The Federalist*, "For why declare that things shall not be done which there is no power to do?"

But the opposition raised the fear that in the face of the powerful new federal government, state government would come to mean very little. If the states got swallowed up as political entities, the states would no longer be able to protect the people's rights.

Article V
We the people of the United States . . . . [the "Members' Edition" of the Constitution], Philadelphia, 1787.

Article 5 of the new Constitution provided for the orderly amendment process that made possible the addition of the Bill of Rights —the first ten amendments— two years later.

The Constitution was signed on September 17, 1787. Shown here is Article 5 in the "Members' Edition" of the Constitution, printed for the members of the Constitutional Convention immediately after adoption.

Today, television provides a forum for public debate on issues and candidates. How would Ted Koppel handle the Federalist/Anti-Federalist debates?

39

The Constitution was to be ratified by special conventions called for the purpose in the states. The big states of Virginia, Pennsylvania, New York and Massachusetts were crucial. The Federalists managed to rush ratification through the Pennsylvania convention in December 1787. Massachusetts followed in January 1788.

But it was hardly smooth sailing for the Federalists. In Pennsylvania the opposition remained united in defeat and issued their "dissent"—a minority report proposing 15 amendments for a federal bill of rights. The minority said that such a measure was "indispensable to . . . 'those inalienable and personal' rights of man." In Massachusetts the ratifying convention itself called, officially, for a federal declaration of rights. Eventually, four more states, including the pivotal New York and Virginia, would ratify with a call for a bill of rights.

In many ways the Virginia ratifying convention was the key test for the Constitution. Virginia was the largest and most powerful state. It was also home to some preeminent American statesmen, Washington, Jefferson, Madison, Mason and Patrick Henry among them. In no other state was the opposition to the Constitution so formidable. In Virginia, the Federalists found Mason, Henry and Richard Henry Lee allied against them.

James Madison naturally took charge of the task of winning ratification in Virginia. Mason and Henry led the opposition, and as the convention opened in June 1788, the two factions seemed evenly matched. The Virginia Federalists were already persuaded that they would have to go along with recommendations for a bill of rights to secure ratification. But this concession did not go far enough for the opposition. Patrick Henry and his allies held out for "previous amendment." That is, they wanted the addition of protections of rights to the Constitution *before* Virginia would ratify. They suggested this

might even be done in cooperation with other states. This might require the convening of a second constitutional convention, something the Federalists wanted desperately to avoid. So it was promised that if Virginia ratified, the new Congress would take up the issue of a federal declaration of rights.

The compromise proved sufficient—ratification passed with a few votes to spare. After voting, the Virginia convention remained in session to draft a series of amendments for the consideration of the new Congress. The list of articles offered the substance of eight of the ten amendments which would eventually make up the United States Bill of Rights.

About a month after the Virginia convention, New York ratified the Constitution, the 11th state to do so. America was going to have a new government and the issue of the bill of rights shifted to the floor of the House of Representatives in the First U.S. Congress.

George Mason's Objections to the Bill of Rights - to George Washington.

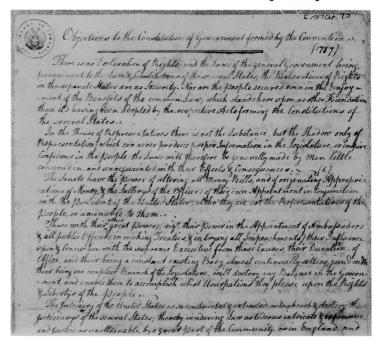

40

George Mason:
America's
Forgotten Founder

George Mason, by Dominic W. Boudet after the lost 1750 original by John Hesselius. Courtesy, the Virginia Museum of Fine Arts, Richmond.

George Mason (1725-1792) has been called "The Reluctant Statesman;" "The Man who Wouldn't Sign;" and "The Forgotten Founding Father." In 1776 he drafted the Virginia Declaration of Rights, the principal source for the federal Bill of Rights—the first ten amendments to the Constitution.

Mason is known only by this single portrait done at the time of his marriage in 1750. He was 25 years old.

George Mason was born on Mason's Neck on the Potomac's Virginia shore in 1725. He died there 67 years later, at Gunston Hall, the exquisite mansion house he had built at the heart of his 5000-acre plantation. In 1792, the year Mason died, George Washington was presiding in Philadelphia over the Federal Government of the new United States of America. In times gone by Washington and Mason had been friends and neighbors. But Mason's opposition to the Constitution had ended their long friendship; Washington now spoke of Mason as his former friend. When news of the death at Gunston Hall reached Philadelphia, the President, and the nation as a whole, scarcely seemed to notice. That silence demonstrated the eclipse of George Mason's reputation as one of the principal architects of our national government, an eclipse which the passage of time would deepen.

In Mason's own time Americans understood his importance as the statesman who drafted the Virginia Declaration of Rights. Thomas Jefferson remembered Mason as "one of our really great men and of the first order of greatness."

Mason's Virginia Declaration had influenced Jefferson's Declaration of Independence. In the months and years to come, that influence continued. The Declaration of Rights and the Constitution of Virginia were copied by many of the other American colonies after the break with Britain compelled them to recreate their state governments. The most notable offspring of Mason's Declaration of Rights is of course the federal Bill of Rights. But in 1789, the same year our Bill of Rights was drafted, the French

Revolution broke out and Mason's words found new expression in Paris in the Declaration of the Rights of Man. In this century those words shaped the United Nations' Declaration of Human Rights. Mason's contribution to the cause of human liberty is a remarkable achievement, all the more remarkable for the obscurity in which the great constitutionalist remains shrouded. As Mason's biographer, Robert Rutland, has observed, "few documents have ever had such a wide impact on society and yet brought so little public recognition for the principal author as the Virginia Declaration of Rights."

In the summer of 1787 Mason traveled to Philadelphia to attend the Constitutional Convention. It was the longest trip of his life and the only time he ever ventured outside the borders of his beloved Virginia. That did not deter him, however, from making his presence felt on the floor at Independence Hall. Mason was one of the handful of delegates who commanded the debates. But on September 12, as the weary delegates could finally look forward to the end of the Convention, Mason called for a bill of rights to be added to the nearly-finished Constitution. It was voted down. A week later, George Mason and two other delegates refused to sign the completed Constitution.

In the struggle to ratify the Constitution, the Federalists were forced to acknowledge their mistake in omitting a bill of rights. They prevailed only with promises to amend the Constitution with guarantees of individual liberties. Madison shepherded the Bill of Rights amendments through Congress in the summer of 1789. Far removed from the seat of government, Mason followed these developments with an understandable interest. "I have received much Satisfaction from the Amendments to the federal Constitution. . . . I cou'd chearfully put my Hand & Heart to the new Government," he wrote in marked contrast to his angry vow to chop that hand off.

During the Revolution, Mason had said, "If I can only live to see the American Union firmly fixed, and free government well established in our Western World, and can leave to my children but a Crust of Bread and Liberty, I shall die satisfied." With the Bill of Rights joined forever to the Constitution, we may imagine that George Mason did indeed get his wish.

Question
Authority

peachments of Officers of the United States; to all cases of Admiralty and Maritime Jurisdiction; to Controversies between two or more States (except such as shall regard Territory or Jurisdiction) between a State and citizens of another State, between citizens of different States, and between a State or the citizens thereof and foreign States, citizens or subjects. In cases of Impeachment, cases affecting Ambassadors, other Public Ministers and Consuls, and those in which a State shall be party, this Jurisdiction shall be original. In all the other cases beforementioned it shall be appellate, with such exceptions and under such regulations as the Legislature shall make. The Legislature may assign any part of the jurisdiction abovementioned (except the trial of the President of the United States) in the manner and under the limitations which it shall think proper, to such Inferior Courts as it shall constitute from time to time.

Sect. 4. The trial of all criminal offences (except in cases of impeachments) shall be in the State where they shall be committed; and shall be by jury.

Sect. 5. Judgment, in cases of Impeachment, shall not extend further than to removal from office, and disqualification to hold and enjoy any office of honour, trust or profit under the United States. But the party convicted shall nevertheless be liable and subject to indictment, trial, judgment and punishment, according to law.

XI.

No State shall coin money; nor grant letters of marque and reprisal; nor enter into any treaty, alliance, or confederation; nor grant any title of nobility.

XII.

No State, without the consent of the Legislature of the United States, shall emit bills of credit, or make any thing but specie a tender in payment of debts; lay imposts or duties on imports; nor keep troops or ships of war in time of peace; nor enter into any agreement or compact with another State, or with any foreign power; nor engage in any war, unless it shall be actually invaded by enemies, or the danger of invasion be so imminent, as not to admit of a delay, until the Legislature of the United States can be consulted.

XIV.

The citizens of each State shall be entitled to all privileges and immunities of citizens in the several States.

XV.

Any person charged with treason, felony, or high-misdemeanor in any State, who shall flee from justice, and shall be found in any other State, shall, on demand of the Executive Power of the State from which he fled, be delivered up and removed to the State having jurisdiction of the offence.

XVI.

Full faith shall be given in each State to the acts of the Legislatures, and to the records and judicial proceedings of the courts and magistrates of every other State.

XVII.

New States lawfully constituted or established within the limits of the United States may be admitted, by the Legislature, into this government; but to such admission the consent of two-thirds of the Members present in each House shall be necessary. If a new State shall arise within the limits of any of the present States, the consent of the Legislatures of such States shall be also necessary to its admission. If the admission be consented to, the new States shall be admitted on the same terms with the original States. But the Legislature may make conditions with the new States concerning the public debt, which shall be then subsisting.

XVII.

CHAPTER 5

THE BILL OF RIGHTS

In the spring of 1789, the first Congress of the United States under the new Constitution met in New York. The Representatives and Senators from the various states had their work cut out for them. The Constitution, though elegant in its simplicity, was little more than a rough outline for government. It would be the job of the legislature to work out the details of how the government would really work.

For many members of the first Congress, the creation of a bill of rights, as had been demanded by a number of state ratifying conventions, seemed a low priority. They thought that the Congress had more important tasks, especially passing measures to raise revenue such as import and tonnage duties. Others saw the need to establish the federal bureaucracy including the departments of State, War and the Treasury. The creation of the federal judiciary was another pressing matter.

Politics, as always, played its part. Anti-Federalists, those who opposed the new Constitution, ironically were not anxious to see a bill of rights proposed, even though they had used its lack as a powerful weapon during the ratification debates. In truth they did not want to lose this weapon in bargaining for greater state power. If a bill of rights were passed, they would be hard pressed to whip up popular opposition to the Federal Government. All in all, the idea of spending time on amending the Constitution before the original plan of government was in force, fell on apathetic ears.

Yet, a bill of rights had one important champion. James Madison, the Virginia Congressman, took it upon himself to keep the issue of the bill of rights on the legislative agenda—this in spite of the fact that he had originally opposed it. He, like many of his Federalist friends, did not think a bill of rights was necessary. He thought the safeguards built into the Constitution itself would protect the people's rights. Besides, Madison also questioned whether a bill of rights would even work. He doubted that a "paper barrier" would stop lawmakers, bowing to the popular will, from passing oppressive laws, especially in times of war or crisis. Still, by the time of the first Congress, Madison had become convinced that a bill of rights would do more good than harm. It could help silence critics of the new constitutional system and give the government a chance to work.

So Madison became the champion of the measure he had at first opposed—a national bill of rights. Madison's had been a sincere conversion. But it was also one much influenced by political realities.

In Virginia, Patrick Henry and his allies had succeeded in denying Madison a seat in the U.S. Senate and had nearly brought about his defeat in a tough campaign for the House. The most potent charge they leveled against Madison was that he, the arch-federalist, still opposed a bill of rights. But candidate Madison had reconsidered and could honestly declare that

"It is my sincere opinion that the Constitution ought to be revised, and that the first Congress meeting under it, ought to prepare and recommend to the states for ratification, the most satisfactory provisions for all essential rights . . . ."

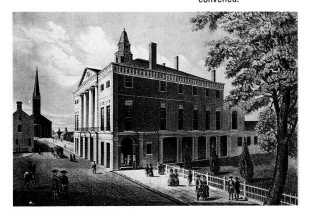

Madison had been influenced by the persuasive arguments of his friend Thomas Jefferson, who wrote from Paris "that a bill of rights is what the people are entitled to against every government on earth." He had also witnessed first hand the strong attachment the people retained for a bill of rights. And he had decided that it could serve to strengthen the authority of republican government, while giving the courts new powers to protect individual liberties. James Madison had carried the Constitution on his shoulders for a long time now. He now came to the first Congress prepared to correct the greatest omission in its framing.

Madison began by compiling amendments. Eight of the 11 states that made up the new government (Rhode Island and North Carolina had not yet joined the Union) had ratified with proposals for amending the Constitution. In all, more than 200 amendments had been offered by the state conventions or by the dissenting minorities of those conventions.

But the task of rescuing a few essential protections from that mass of proposals was not as daunting as it might have seemed; there was considerable agreement on a handful of important propositions. Madison set to work winnowing out proposals which would be difficult to ratify, as well as those which were designed to weaken the central government rather than protect individual rights. At the same time, Madison continued to press the House to consider the proposed amendments. By pure determination he finally got the legislators to agree to consider his proposals for the bill of rights. Though put off before, this time Madison would not take no for an answer.

On the 8th of June 1789, James Madison took the floor of the House of Representatives to propose amending the new Constitution with a bill of rights. "It cannot be a secret to the gentlemen in this House," Madison began, "that, notwithstanding the ratification of this system of Government . . . there is a great number of our constituents who are dissatisfied with it . . . . We ought not to disregard their inclination, but, on the principles of amity and moderation, conform to their wishes, and expressly declare the great rights of mankind secured under this constitution."

Madison proposed a preamble and nine amendments to be incorporated into the body of the Constitution. One of his amendments—the Fourth—was of the greatest importance. It was in itself a ten-clause declaration of rights covering nearly all of the liberties that would find protection in the Bill of Rights. Running through the list, Madison's and the republic's debt to George Mason's Virginia Declaration of Rights is clear. In language that would be largely retained in the Bill of Rights, Madison's inclusive fourth article offered freedom of religion, speech, press and assembly. It also covered the right to bear arms and protection from quartering of troops. It contained protections from unreasonable searches and seizures, excessive bails and fines, and cruel and unusual punishments. Finally, the all-purpose Fourth guaranteed the right to due process and to a speedy public trial.

The preamble Madison offered was also adopted from the Virginia Declaration of Rights. It was a simple "declaration, that all power is originally vested in, and consequently derived from, the people," who retained always the right to change or replace the government under which they had agreed to live. Madison did make one significant departure in the language of the Declaration of Rights — "ought" and "ought not" was changed to read "shall" and "shall not" in the Bill of Rights.

Some of the other elements of Madison's plan are less familiar. He proposed a pair of articles defining Congressional representation and pay, and another limiting the right to bring law suits against the government. These three measures were not ratified by the states.

Federal Hall in New York City where the First Congress convened.

James
Madison:
"Father
of the
Bill
of
Rights"

**James Madison by
Charles Willson Peale,
c. 1792. Courtesy,
Thomas Gilcrease
Institute of American
History and Art, Tulsa,
Oklahoma.**

James Madison
(1751-1836), the "father"
of the Constitution and
the Bill of Rights.

The first of the 11 children of a prosperous Virginia tobacco planter, James Madison was born in March 1751. He was one of the younger members of the extraordinary generation of statesmen that Virginia gave the republic. In the year Madison was born, George Mason was already 26 years old, Washington was 19, and Thomas Jefferson a boy of 8. Madison shared a common heritage with these men, one of solid privilege rooted in the colony's ancient trinity of land, slaves and tobacco. But James Madison's life changed from the common pattern when he left Virginia to attend the College of New Jersey, now known as Princeton University.

From an early age Madison had distinguished himself as a scholar. He read voraciously all his life: history, philosophy, literature, natural history, law and theology. And he could read in Latin, Greek, Hebrew, French, Spanish and Italian. He collected books, extracted notes and passages from them, cataloged and arranged them. He longed throughout a lasting public career to return to a life of quiet study at Montpelier, his elegant home in the foothills of the Blue Ridge Mountains. Such retirement was not soon in coming. For although so sickly as a young man that he predicted he could not "expect a long or healthy life," Madison was to attain the age of 85 and to serve as Secretary of State and fourth President of the United States. Indeed, evidence of James Madison's remarkable vigor of mind are preserved in the Constitution and the Bill of Rights. He has been called "the father" of both those American charters.

He earned his BA at college in only two years by means of what he called "an indiscrete experiment of the minimum of sleep & the maximum of application." Madison then came home to Virginia, where he passed a few years in "feeble health," and studied the law, though without any strong inclination towards a legal career. Then suddenly the sound of gunfire at Lexington and Concord launched James Madison on his life's work.

"On the commencement of the dispute with Great Britain," he recalled in an autobiographical sketch written 60 years later, "[I] entered with the prevailing zeal into the American Cause; being under very early and strong impressions in favour of Liberty both Civil & Religious . . . ." It was "in the spring of 1776," Madison continued, that he "was initiated into the political career by . . . election to the [Virginia] convention, which formed the original Constitution of the State with the Declaration of Rights . . . and which instructed her deputies in [the Continental] Congress to propose final separation from G. Britain . . . ."

This was an initiation indeed. The 25-year-old scholar found himself a member of the celebrated Virginia Convention, which counted as its achievements drafting the Virginia Declaration of Rights and the state's new constitution, and making the momentous decision to break once and for all with Britain.

In this first appearance upon the public stage, Madison exhibited a characteristic devotion to civil liberties when he moved for an important change in George Mason's clause on religious toleration in the Declaration of Rights. Mason, as Madison remembered it, "had inadvertently adopted the word *toleration*." The change that Madison suggested and the convention agreed to ". . . declared the freedom of conscience to be a *natural and absolute right*." The distinction between religious *toleration* and religious *freedom* is an important one. Toleration was governmental permission for dissenters to practice religions other than an established state church. Religious freedom, on the other hand, was no gift from the powers that be, but rather a fundamental human right.

At the Virginia Convention in 1776, young Madison had managed to impress some weighty company. He was given a post in the state government where he soon became the friend of Virginia's governor, Thomas Jefferson. It was the beginning of the most fruitful political collaboration in American history. The beginning of the Jefferson-Madison collaboration can also be seen as the birth of the Democratic-Republican party which would dominate national politics throughout the republic's early years. Its reign lasted from the election of Thomas Jefferson in 1800 through the end of James Monroe's presidency in 1825.

In 1780 Madison assumed national responsibilities for the first time when he took a seat in the Continental Congress in Philadelphia. He served through the end of the Revolution. In the process he learned first hand about the weaknesses of the Articles of Confederation as a basis for national government.

By this time, Madison had devoted himself completely to the cause of liberty and to the proposition that an American republic could lead the world to a new and enlightened era of self-government. But first the republic needed an effective national government. Madison set to work to see that it got one. Madison carried the Constitution of the United States on his shoulders and in his head for years. He was the moving spirit behind the Mount Vernon (George Washington's home) Conference in 1785 and the Annapolis Convention in 1786. The two preliminary meetings resulted in the Constitutional Convention.

Madison had prepared with his usual diligence. He had asked Jefferson to buy for him in Paris "rare and valuable books" that might "throw light on the general constitution . . . of the several confederacies that have existed." From his readings he filled up a notebook he titled "Of Ancient and Modern Confederacies." James Madison dominated the Convention. Another delegate left a good quick sketch of the 36-year-old philosopher-statesman which began, *"Mr. Madison is a character who has long been in public life; and what is very remarkable every person seems to acknowledge his greatness. He blends together the profound politician with the Scholar. In the management of every great question he evidently took the lead in the Convention . . . ."*

But Madison failed to lead on the issue of a national bill of rights. A few days before the Convention ended, the delegates made the mistake of voting down George Mason's proposal to include a declaration of rights. It was all that James Madison and the Federalists could do to secure the Constitution's ratification.

At the crucial Virginia ratifying convention in June 1788, the leading spokesmen for and against the Constitution were Madison and Patrick Henry. The two offered an interesting contrast. It was observed that Henry could keep an audience spellbound for hours, but that afterwards his listeners had trouble remembering what he had said. Madison, on the other hand, spoke so softly it was hard to hear him across the room. He offered no verbal fireworks. But when Madison took his seat, the audience could retrace the progression of his reasoned arguments. In the end, Virginia ratified the Constitution, 89 to 79.

It was during the ratification contest that Madison made his most original contribution to constitutional theory. He argued that self-government could thrive in an extended republic *because,* not in spite of, such a nation's size and diversity. Most of history's classical republics had been city-states small enough for the citizens to gather together to govern themselves. The prevailing theory held that a large nation—and the American states comprised a very large nation indeed—could be ruled only by a despotic government strong enough to extend its powers across the distances. But Madison argued in the pages of *The Federalist* that in America all the authority of government would be derived from the people, from the society. ". . . The society itself will be broken into so many parts, interests and classes of citizens, that the rights of individuals, or of the minority, will be in little danger . . . ," he wrote.

It was also during the ratification struggle that Madison reconsidered his stand on a national bill of rights. He learned, as he said in his speech introducing the Bill of Rights amendments in Congress on June 8, 1789,

> that the great mass of the people who opposed [the Constitution], disliked it because it did not contain effectual provisions against the encroachments on particular rights . . . , nor ought we to consider them safe, while a great number of our fellow-citizens think these securities necessary.

James Madison was now fully convinced that

> "We ought . . . [to] expressly declare the great rights of mankind secured under this constitution."

Letter from Jefferson to Madison— Fifth page —famous quote—"A bill of rights is what all the people on earth are entitled to.

46

A MAP of
the moft INHABITED part of
VIRGINIA
containing the whole PROVINCE of
MARYLAND
with Part of
PENSILVANIA, NEW JERSEY AND NORTH CAROLINA
Drawn by
Joshua Fry & Peter Jefferson
in 1751.

To the Right Honourable, George Dunk Earl of Halifax, First Lord Commiſſioner, and to the Reſt of the Right Honourable and Honourable Commiſſioners for TRADE and PLANTATIONS. This Map is most humbly Inscribed to their Lordships, By their Lordships, Most Obedient & most devoted humble Serv.: Jbo.: Jefferys.

"A Map of the Inhabited part of Virginia, . . . by Joshua Fry and Peter Jefferson," London 1751.

Many of the principal founders of the United States—including Virginians like Washington, Jefferson, Mason and Madison—were born into a world in which slavery had been woven into the fabric of society for generations.

The cartouche of the Jefferson-Fry Map shows half-naked slaves attending prosperous tobacco planters in some London artist's notion of a Virginia port.

Of greater significance, however, were two other proposals which were the work of Madison alone. The first made explicit the separation of powers in the Constitution's definition of a government of executive, legislative and judicial branches. No branch, it said, could exercise the powers assigned to another branch. Even more controversial, because it sought to limit the power of the states, was the provision that

"No State shall violate the equal rights of conscience, or the freedom of the press, or the trial by jury in criminal cases."

Both of these measures would die in Senate debate later that summer.

(The idea of giving the central government power to protect the rights of citizens against encroachments by the states finally became the law of the land in two of the "Civil War Amendments." The Fourteenth (1868) stated that "No State shall make or enforce any law which shall abridge the privileges or immunities of citizens of the United States," nor deny them due process. The Fifteenth (1870) extended federal protection to the right to vote.)

Another of Madison's ideas did survive. To address the concern that only rights listed in the amendments would be protected, Madison proposed what would become the Ninth Amendment: "The enumeration in the Constitution, of certain rights, shall not be construed to deny or disparage others retained by the people."

After debate in the House, Madison's collection of amendments was passed, redrafted as 17 articles. One significant change placed the amendments as a list at the end of the Constitution, rather than weaving them into its text as Madison had wished. This assured that the Bill of Rights would stand as a charter in its own right. It also made the ten amendments memorable as the republic's catalog of liberties.

Next the Senate had its turn. After further delay, a conference of both Houses prepared the agreed upon text of the twelve amendments to send to the states for ratification on September 25, 1789.

Appropriately it was the ratification on December 15, 1791 by Virginia—home of Madison, Mason and Jefferson—that made the Bill of Rights an organic part of the Constitution, the supreme law of the United States of America.

JOHN MARSHALL AND THE POWER OF JUDICIAL REVIEW

Though the Bill of Rights was ratified, it had little immediate effect. The country concentrated on economic recovery and expansion. The new government was preoccupied with creating the mechanisms for running the nation, determining what powers each of the branches should have, and fears of international conflict, first with Britain and then with France.

The French Revolution of 1789 did briefly bring the issue of rights to the forefront. The Federalists feared that the violent bloodletting and calls for "liberty, equality, and fraternity" which marked the overthrow of the French monarchy, might spread to America. These fears became more real when Napoleon came to power and his conquering armies spread and imposed the Revolutionary ideas across Europe. The events of the 1790s also brought large numbers of French radicals to the United States eager to share their ideas. In response, the Federalist-controlled Congress passed the Alien and Sedition Acts in 1798 to expel French "agents" from the United States and make anti-government speech and press a crime. Federalist appointed judges were more than willing to convict people accused under the statutes.

Justice Marshall falls from ladder in law library and gasps, "I was floored."

In response, the state legislatures of Virginia and Kentucky passed resolutions drafted by Madison and Jefferson respectively, declaring the federal acts unconstitutional. While the Federal Government arguably had the constitutional power to pass the Alien Act, the First Amendment denied Congress the power to abridge free speech or a free press. In declaring the acts invalid, Kentucky and Virginia asserted a claim to states' rights which would erupt many times in American history. The Alien and Sedition crisis passed when the Federalists lost the presidency and Congress in the elections of 1800. But, the issue of the meaning of the First Amendment, especially in times of war or crisis, was not resolved and would come up again in future years.

This episode also demonstrated the weakness of the U.S. Supreme Court. It had little power or prestige. Packed with Federalist justices, it could hardly have been expected to overturn the acts of a Federalist congress or president and was more interested in increasing federal power than in restricting it. One Federalist-appointed Chief Justice, the fourth, changed all that. His name was John Marshall.

Marshall took office in 1801, appointed by President Adams. He won Senate approval only by a very narrow margin. Most expected him, like his predecessors, to serve only a short time. But when he retired in 1835, the Supreme Court had taken its place as a branch of government equal to the others. Marshall's chance to prove himself and the Court came with the case of *Marbury v. Madison* in 1803.

William Marbury had been appointed a justice of the peace in the District of Columbia by President Adams in the last hours of his administration. Unfortunately, the appointment was not delivered to him by the time Adams left office. The new president, Thomas Jefferson ordered the then Secretary of State, James Madison, not to deliver the appointment. Yet, the Judiciary Act of 1789 had given the Supreme Court the power to order judges and government officials to act. Marbury, relying on this law, sued to get his appointment.

Marshall, in his famous opinion, agreed that Marbury had a right to the appointment. He ruled, however, that the Supreme Court did not have the power to order Madison to deliver it and make it official. The section of the Judiciary Act in question, he determined, violated the Constitution by giving the Supreme Court a power it did not have. He went on to hold that when a law conflicts with the Constitution, it is the duty of the Supreme Court to overturn it. In giving up one power, Marshall carved out for the Court, a much greater one: the power of judicial review.

Yet, the Supreme Court under Marshall would not use this power to expand individual rights. In fact, near the end of his service on the Court, a case arose that would put the Bill of Rights to sleep until after the Civil War. In the case of *Barron v. Baltimore* in 1833, the aging John Marshall wrote an opinion which ruled that the Bill of Rights could not be used to invalidate a state law or action. States were free to pass laws forbidding free speech or upholding slavery, and the federal courts were powerless to stop them. Only state constitutions and courts could provide a remedy. Not until the 20th century would the Supreme Court, using the power of judicial review, rediscover the Bill of Rights.

John Marshall, circa 1808.

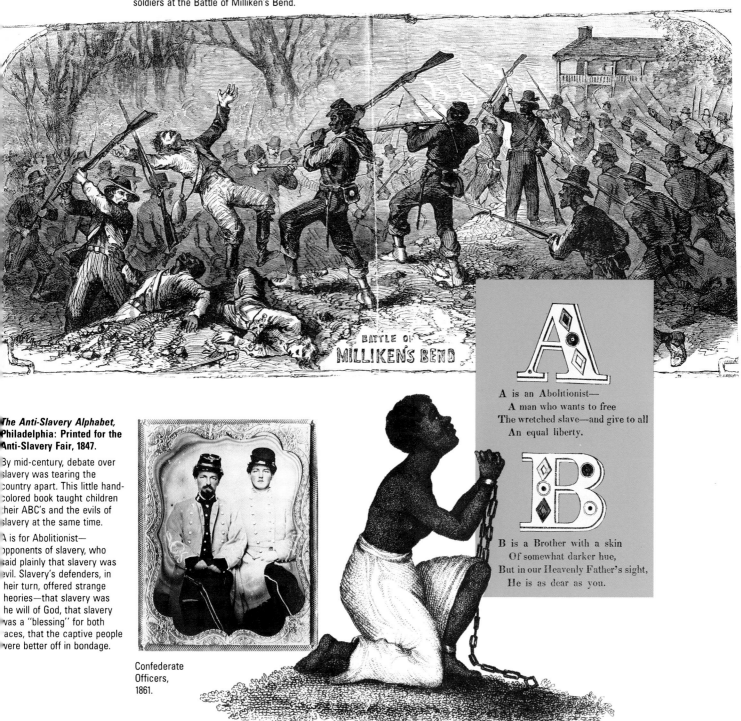

Black regiment fighting white Confederate soldiers at the Battle of Milliken's Bend.

BATTLE OF MILLIKEN'S BEND

A is an Abolitionist—
A man who wants to free
The wretched slave—and give to all
An equal liberty.

B is a Brother with a skin
Of somewhat darker hue,
But in our Heavenly Father's sight,
He is as dear as you.

**The Anti-Slavery Alphabet,
Philadelphia: Printed for the
Anti-Slavery Fair, 1847.**

By mid-century, debate over slavery was tearing the country apart. This little hand-colored book taught children their ABC's and the evils of slavery at the same time.

A is for Abolitionist—opponents of slavery, who said plainly that slavery was evil. Slavery's defenders, in their turn, offered strange theories—that slavery was the will of God, that slavery was a "blessing" for both races, that the captive people were better off in bondage.

Confederate Officers, 1861.

Engraved by P. Reason,

A Colored Young Man of the City of New York. 1835

49

THE CIVIL WAR

Only about seventy-five years, a single lifetime, separated the adoption of the Constitution and the passage of the Constitution's 13th Amendment that outlawed slavery in the United States forever in 1865. By every measure—population, wealth, territory—the nation had grown enormously in that lifetime. Pacing the nation's growth had been the rise of American slavery. There were about 650,000 slaves in 1787; more than four million in 1865. By the outbreak of the Civil War, the territory of the slave states was greater than all the 13 colonies in 1776. Attitudes towards slavery had also changed. If many of the republic's founders had been slaveowners, few of them could have been described as defenders of slavery. Men like Washington, Jefferson, Madison and Mason hated slavery, but they saw no immediate prospect for bringing it to an end. They hoped that slavery was destined for a natural extinction.

As the nation aged, debate on slavery grew more heated. Nothing fueled the debate as much as the country's westward expansion. Territorial expansion was a dynamic central to American nationhood. In the lifetime between the Constitution and the Civil War the territory of the United States grew fourfold. Each new state admitted to the Union threatened to upset the political balance of power between the slave and free states. A series of Congressional compromises over the admission of new states served to postpone a showdown between the free and slave factions in the United States.

But by the middle of the 19th century American slavery was attacked and defended with rising anger. The uncompromising opponents of slavery—the abolitionists—were perceived as radical by many Americans. They said plainly that slavery was evil; sometimes they said the slaveowners were evil too. Many abolitionists were willing to break the law to fight slavery. Some of them called the Constitution a "covenant with death," and preached "no union with slaveowners." Slavery's defenders in their turn twisted reason to brace up strange theories—that slavery was the will of God, that slavery was a "blessing" for both races, that the liberty and equality white Southerners were presumed to enjoy rested on the condition of the submerged class of people who had no rights at all. There is of course little evidence that the black people of the South were ever persuaded by such ideas as these. They had been resisting their enslavement for decades and quickly saw that the Civil War was the chance to seize their freedom.

By the time Abraham Lincoln challenged Stephen A. Douglas for the Senate in 1858, it had become clear that the founders' hopes for a peaceful end to slavery was not to be. In the most famous of his debates with Douglas, Lincoln eloquently expressed the fears of many when he predicted that a crisis was now inevitable:

"A house divided against itself cannot stand."
I believe that this government cannot endure, permanently half slave and half free.
I do not expect the Union to be dissolved—I do not expect the house to fall—but I do expect it will cease to be divided.
It will become all one thing, or all the other.

Abraham Lincoln thought his second inaugural address his finest literary creation. Delivered March 4, 1865, just six weeks before his murder, the brief speech

Abraham Lincoln before he became President.

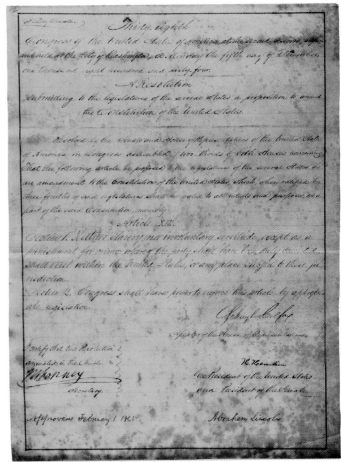

Abraham Lincoln, autograph manuscript, pocket notebook with handwritten and newspaper excerpts from his speeches in the Lincoln-Douglas debates. 1858.

By the time Abraham Lincoln and Stephen A. Douglas contended for the U.S. Senate in 1858, the nation had nearly reached the end of compromises; the final tragic crisis over slavery was at hand.

Lincoln lost the Senate election to Douglas. He prepared this outline of his positions on the issue of "negro equality" for the use of a supporter during the campaign. In the opening displayed here, Lincoln said that

". . . I think the negro is included in the word 'men' used in the Declaration of Independence . . . ."

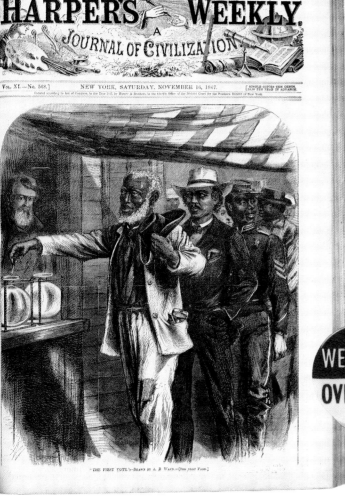

The 13th Amendment to the Constitution, abolishing slavery in the United States, souvenir copy signed by Abraham Lincoln, Vice President Hannibal Hamlin and others, dated 12 February 1865.

The 13th Amendment completed the destruction of slavery begun by the Emancipation Proclamation.

Lincoln is known to have signed about a dozen such souvenir copies of the 13th Amendment.

is best remembered for its final sentence beginning, "With malice toward none; with charity toward all . . . ." But before reaching that soaring call for national reconciliation, Lincoln revealed what he had come to see as the meaning of the terrible civil war which had passed over the land in the four years since he had first sworn the oath to defend the Constitution of the United States.

Abraham Lincoln's anguished reflections on his country's ordeal had sent him looking for comfort in that old human trick of imagining that suffering has a meaning, a purpose and an end. Lincoln found that meaning in slavery and the justice of God:

> *Slavery was a crime and the crime of slavery lay at the heart of the war. All Americans, north and south, shared in the guilt. It was upon all of them that God had visited His terrible punishment.*

In the second inaugural address, Lincoln reckoned the cost thus:

> *Fondly do we hope—fervently do we pray—that this mighty scourge of war may speedily pass away. Yet, if God wills that it continue until all the wealth piled up by the bondsman's two hundred and fifty years of unrequited toil shall be sunk, and until every drop of blood drawn with the lash shall be paid by another drawn by the sword, as was said three thousand years ago, so it still must be said, "The judgments of the Lord are true and righteous altogether."*

Lincoln understood that slavery was the tragic flaw that united, as well as divided, all Americans. Slavery was the dark reverse of the coin of liberty the founders had bequeathed the republic. Those men remained the most brilliant generation of statesmen the nation had brought forth. The revolution they made had changed the history of the world. But their revolution's noble principles were mocked by the continuation of human slavery in the new country. They could find no solution even within the sweep of their vision. In the end they had made an enormous compromise. It could not be hidden by the Constitution's vast silence, with its handful of oblique references to "Persons held to Service or Labour" and its outlawing of the African slave trade in 20 years.

If slavery was the republic's original sin, redemption extracted a fearsome price. The Civil War ransomed some four million black Americans from their ancestral captivity only after four years of the most deadly fighting. More than 600,000 American soldiers lost their lives, yielding the grim ratio of one man destroyed for every six people the war set free. That these casualties were inflicted on a population of only 32 million assured that the waves of grief and desolation washed over every part of the land. Even after more than a hundred years and two great world wars, the number of Civil War dead still exceeds the total, combined losses in every other war the United States has ever fought. And that war cost billions of dollars at a time when 20 U.S. dollars bought an ounce of gold. ("Slave property" alone had been valued at two to three billion dollars in 1860.) Lincoln had known that the nation would suffer terribly.

Abraham Lincoln hated slavery. "If slavery is not wrong, nothing is wrong," he said, but he accepted that as the founders' dilemma. He knew that the Constitution they had framed gave the Federal Government no power to interfere with slavery in those states where it had taken root. He held to this principle for nearly all of his political life and for about half his presidency. Although it was a calculated political statement, Lincoln could hardly have been more clear when he said that his "paramount object in this struggle is to save the Union, and is not either to save or to destroy slavery . . . ." Before the war, Lincoln had believed, like many others in the new Republican party, that the government could do no more than exclude slavery from new states and territories. Then they hoped that, confined to the South, the peculiar institution would dwindle towards a natural extinction.

The war changed all that.

Confederate Colonel
John Mosley and his men.

Black Union
Infantry
Corporal.

Jim Crow laws finally come to an end
when the people refused to obey
them in the 1950s and 60s here at a
lunch counter.

Roger
Brooke
Taney

Roger Brooke Taney was born in 1777, the year after
the Declaration of Independence was signed. He
died in October 1864, when the most celebrated
assertion of that document—that all men are created
equal—was being vindicated by the force of arms.

The Supreme Court had a Southern, proslavery
majority in 1857. Chief Justice Taney in particular
believed that the South's way of life was threatened
by abolitionism and by growing Northern power.
Taney was devoted to the defense of what he saw
as his section's rights. First among those rights was
the preservation of slavery. He saw any attempt by
outsiders to tamper with slavery, or to seek to
restrict its spread into the territories as infringement
on the rights of property. During the years before
the Dred Scott decision, Taney, like many other
Southerners, became convinced that he was witness to a vast and malignant conspiracy to pervert
the republic the founders had created. He saw, in
the Dred Scott case, the chance to deal a crushing
blow to the antislavery movement. Scott, a slave,
had been taken by his owner to Illinois, a free state
and then back to Missouri, a slave state. Since
he had been a resident of free territory, he sued
for his freedom.

With his ruling in the case, Taney aimed to establish
as law nothing less than the principle that the Constitution protected slavery, denied citizenship to
blacks forever, and gave government no power to
restrict the spread of slavery in the federal territories and the new states which would be created
there.

The reaction to the Court's decision was immediate
and impassioned. Southerners boasted that their
right to slave property was now the law of the land.
Republicans and other opponents of slavery thought
not. They too saw a great conspiracy operating in
American affairs, a conspiracy to extend and maintain slavery. In his celebrated "house divided"
speech during the Lincoln-Douglas debates,
Abraham Lincoln warned that slavery's advocates
intended to "push it forward, till it shall become
lawful in *all* the States . . . *North* as well as *South.*"
That was a result many in the North refused to
accept. The legislatures of several Northern states
passed resolutions condemning the Dred Scott decision. Republicans announced their determination
to win the presidency in 1860 and overturn the
decision in a reorganized Supreme Court.

It had long been an article of faith for many mode-
rate opponents of slavery that, confined to the Old
South, slavery would gradually die out, without
upheaval or bloodshed. They had been willing to
stand aside and wait for such an outcome. Now it
appeared that slavery had to be vigorously attacked.
Rather than resolving the crisis over slavery, Judge
Taney's decision in *Dred Scott v. Sandford* (1857),
had brought the nation's two opposing factions
closer than ever to political stalemate.

Judge Taney died just before Lincoln's re-election
in 1864, not knowing the outcome of the great Civil
War then raging across the land. Perhaps he did
know that his attempt to defend the South and its
way of life with the Dred Scott decision had has-
tened the coming of the cataclysm which was
sweeping the old South away.

Roger Brooke Taney.

53

On the first day of 1863, President Lincoln issued the Emancipation Proclamation as a military measure by the "Commander-in-Chief . . . in time of actual armed rebellion against authority and government of the United States . . . ." The Proclamation was part of a strategy to crush the Confederacy without making more enemies in the slave-owning border states. It proved a most powerful weapon of war. Many saw an irony in the President's proclaiming freedom for slaves in only those regions still in rebellion, that is, only in places where the government had not the power to enforce its will. Still, it would not belong before the grand armies of the republic, each trailing its throng of newly-freed people, advanced across the doomed Confederate States of America. More than two years remained until the last Southern army laid down its arms, but the Emancipation Proclamation had already served slavery with a writ of execution. African Americans throughout the South, people who had been working at their own emancipation through generations of escape and resistance, had no doubt at all as to the meaning of the Proclamation.

Article XIII

Section 1. Neither slavery nor involuntary servitude, except as a punishment for crime whereof the party shall have been duly convicted, shall exist within the United States or any place subject to their jurisdiction. Section 2. Congress shall have power to enforce this article by appropriate legislation.

It was the Senate Judiciary Committee, chaired by Illinois Republican Lyman Trumbull, that proposed the actual wording of the 13th Amendment. But the resolution echoes the language Thomas Jefferson had used in the Northwest Ordinance of 1787 to outlaw slavery in the Ohio Valley wilderness.

The 13th Amendment sailed through the Republican-controlled Senate in April 1864. But it wasn't until half a year later, on the last day of January 1865, that the House passed the resolution and sent it to the states for ratification. Northern victory in the war was now a certainty. That

the courage of tens of thousands of black soldiers with rifles and bayonets had helped assure that victory gave a renewed fervency to the calls for universal emancipation.

History was made on the day the votes were counted and Congress passed the 13th Amendment; everyone knew something very important had happened. A Republican Congressman described the rejoicing beneath the dome of the Capitol:

> *Members joined in the shouting and kept at it for some minutes. Some embraced one another, others wept like children. I have felt, ever since the vote, that I was in a new country . . . .*

The amendment still needed ratification, but no one in the Capitol doubted that slavery had been dealt a death blow in that place and in that hour.

It was not until December 1865 that ratification by three-quarters of the states bound the 13th Amendment to the Constitution, and by then Abraham Lincoln was dead.

While the 13th Amendment ended slavery, it did not guarantee those freed of full participation in American life, the protection of law or the rights of citizenship. In truth, a number of southern states had passed what were called "Black Codes," which were designed to keep blacks in an inferior position. For example, in Mississippi, freed slaves were barred from any business except "husbandry" without a special license and were not allowed to rent property except in towns and cities. The second part of the 13th Amendment did give Congress the right to enforce the end of slavery with "appropriate legislation." In face of the Black Codes, the Congress passed the Freedman's Bureau Bill and the Civil Rights Act of 1866. The latter declared that all persons born in the United States were citizens, except Indians who were not taxed, and outlined certain rights everyone should have. They included the right to make and enforce contracts, to sue, to inherit property, to own and sell property and have the equal benefit and be subject to the same laws as white citizens.

Protester remembers Martin Luther King, 1990.

REGISTER
AND VOTE

NOW THAT WE'VE
EXTENDED OUR VOTING
RIGHTS LETS EXTEND
OUR VOTING "RIGHT"

Supreme Court Outlaws
Segregation in Schools

Dr. Martin Luther King
leads protest march.

Union Soldiers.

55

In this there was a problem. Opponents of the Act, including President Andrew Johnson, pointed out that under the Constitution, only states had the power to define the rights of their citizens. This was not one of the powers granted by the Constitution to the Federal Government. To overcome this constitutional argument, (at the same time Congress was working on the Civil Rights Act) it constructed another amendment to the Constitution: the 14th.

The 14th Amendment declared that all persons born or naturalized in the United States were citizens of the nation and of the state where they lived. The Amendment also placed significant restrictions on the power of the states. "No State shall make or enforce any law which shall abridge the privileges or immunities of citizens of the United States; nor shall any State deprive any person of life, liberty, or property, without due process of law; nor deny to any person within its jurisdiction the equal protection of the laws."

To be re-admitted to statehood, each of the southern states that rebelled during the Civil War would have to ratify this amendment. By 1868, the 14th Amendment was declared to have been ratified and it became the supreme law of the land. In future years, this Amendment more than any other would define and expand the rights of Americans.

But the Republican Congress had not yet finished its work in amending the Constitution. It also wanted to assure that blacks would be able to vote in southern state elections. Once they could vote, reasoned the Congress, elected officials themselves would have to afford them the protections and rights of citizens or fear being removed from office. The amendment read:

"The right of citizens of the United States to vote shall not be denied or abridged by the United States or by any State on account of race, color, or previous condition of servitude."

Again the Congress got the power to enforce the amendment and the rebel states had to ratify it before they could be re-admitted to the Union. The 15th Amendment was finally ratified in 1870.

The scars of the Civil War did not quickly heal, nor did the rights guaranteed by the new amendments erase the 250-year legacy of slavery for those who had suffered under it or for their descendants. Still, the amendments planted seeds that would bloom a century later when the modern civil rights movement would move America closer to the promise of equal protection of law for all.

White supremacy and racism did not end with the Civil War as modern KKK and Nazi members demonstrate.

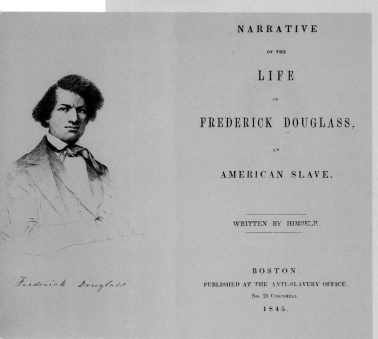

NARRATIVE

OF THE

LIFE

OF

FREDERICK DOUGLASS,

AN

AMERICAN SLAVE.

WRITTEN BY HIMSELF.

BOSTON:
PUBLISHED AT THE ANTI-SLAVERY OFFICE.
No. 25 CORNHILL
1845.

Frederick Douglass

The life of Frederick Douglass, the great African American statesman, encompassed the most momentous years of his people's long history in America. He had been born a slave about 1817 in the slave state of Maryland during the presidency of slaveowner James Monroe. As he grew to manhood, the South's "peculiar institution" was flourishing and slaveowners were beginning to be possessed of a new confidence about the future of a culture based on slavery. When Frederick Douglass died in 1895, slavery had been extinct for 30 years, but his people were still not free, despite the promises of "the Civil War Amendments"—the 13th, 14th and 15th amendments to the Constitution.

Given the name Frederick Augustus Washington Bailey, he started calling himself Douglass to throw off slavehunters after he escaped from bondage. The fugitive slave's first public appearance came in 1841 when he rose to address an audience in Massachusetts. The effect was electrifying. Douglass presented the striking figure of a tall, handsome man possessed of a fine speaking voice, a leonine head and lion's fierce determination to match. Frederick Douglass told the story of his own life in slavery, the brutal treatment he had suffered, his struggle to teach himself to read, his longings for freedom and his two escapes, the second a successful one. The turning point of Douglass' personal history probably came the day he fought back against an overseer bent on whipping him, forcing the man to back off. He learned that resistance was possible, even in slavery. Douglass' account impressed all who heard it and he soon became a paid employee of the Anti-Slavery Society.

When the Civil War came, Douglass rejoiced that the "slaveholders themselves have saved our cause from ruin." He was always a step or two ahead of his time and said from the beginning what many Americans were still unwilling to admit—that slavery was the root cause of the great American conflict. He was contemptuous of Abraham Lincoln's attempts to conciliate the South during the early months of his presidency. Douglass greeted the Emancipation Proclamation, however, as a sign that the war was "... no longer a mere strife for territory or dominion, but a contest of civilization against barbarism."

He had from the start urged that blacks be enlisted as Union soldiers, recognizing not only that such action could hasten Northern victory, but also that it would be more difficult to deny the rights of citizenship to men who had worn the uniform of the United States. Although Northern leaders were at first reluctant, it was not long before black regiments were being fielded. About 180,000 African American men eventually saw service, representing a significant part of the total Union enlistment. Douglass helped recruit some the regiments and he argued against discrimination in pay and duties, and urged retaliation against Confederate murder and enslavement of black prisoners of war.

A few weeks before his death in 1895, Douglass was asked what advice he would give to a young black American. "Agitate! Agitate! Agitate!" the old man answered.

Frederick Douglass.

CHAPTER 7

A CHANGING AMERICA

In the late 19th and early 20th centuries, the history of the Bill of Rights shifted from a focus on the ideas contained in the amendments themselves to their practical meaning to the lives of Americans. The country was changing. Urbanization, industrialization, and immigration created new and often conflicting conditions and ideas. Increasingly, the U.S. Supreme Court was forced to take a larger role in interpreting the Constitution to confront deep divisions in society. Social conflicts existed between the desire of giant corporations to enlarge their profits in the name of "free enterprise" and the struggle of organized labor and social reformers to secure better and safer working conditions. There were economic conflicts between the enactment of elaborate business regulations under the state's "police power" and the call for a "laissez-faire" approach to encourage innovative entrepreneurship. Indeed, the Court itself had conflicts between the competing theories of "judicial activism" and "judicial restraint."

By mediating these debates when posed as constitutional issues, the opinions of the Court became the vehicle for determining the meaning of the Bill of Rights. It is a measure of the heightened pace of judicial review to realize that *before* 1865, the Supreme Court only found two federal and 38 state statutes unconstitutional. Between 1865 and 1899, it struck down 18 federal and 126 state laws.

Acting under the Due Process and Equal Protection provisions of the 14th Amendment, coupled with the doctrine of Freedom of Contract, the Supreme Court repeatedly overturned laws that restricted businesses, regulated working conditions or taxed corporations. In one year, 1895, the Court upheld a federal injunction against striking railroad workers (In re Debs); severely limited the scope of the Sherman Antitrust Act (United States v. E.C. Knight Company) and struck down the federal income tax law (Pollock v. Farmers Loan & Trust). One scholar referred to these decisions as "related aspects of a massive judicial entry into the socioeconomic scene, . . . a conservative oriented revolution."

While the Court busied itself with protecting big business under an expansive interpretation of the 14th Amendment, it turned a deaf ear to those blacks for whom the Amendment had been enacted. In fact, during the last decades of the 19th century, blacks had lost most of what they had gained from the passage of the 14th and 15th amendments. By 1890, many southern states began passing what were known as "Jim Crow laws." These laws segregated blacks from the white population in housing, use of public facilities, in public transportation and in hotels. In *Plessy v. Ferguson* (1896), the Court established the infamous "separate but equal" doctrine, which would permit Jim Crow laws until it was overruled in *Brown v. Board of Education* (1954).

U.S. House of Representatives in session.

New York City Sweatshop.

Child Laborers
and the Court.

CASES AND CONTROVERSIES

Yick Wo v. Hopkins (1886)

The 14th Amendment guaranteed equal protection of the laws to all persons without regard to any difference of race, of color, or of nationality. To fulfill the true meaning of this command, the Supreme Court looks not only at whether laws *on their face* are discriminatory, but also whether *as applied* they violate the 14th Amendment. In 1886, in *Yick Wo v. Hopkins,* the Court confronted a San Francisco ordinance which made it a crime to run a laundry business in any building not made of stone or brick, with such exceptions for wooden structures as city officials might choose to make. Although the law itself said nothing about race or nationality, the officials exercised their discretion in a patently discriminatory fashion. They allowed 80 wooden laundries operated by Caucasians, but rejected 200 applicants of Chinese extraction. In a unanimous opinion by Justice Stanley Matthews, the Court held that the ordinance was applied so unequally and so oppressively that it denied equal protection of the laws. While Asian-Americans would continue to face discrimination, the Chinese who stood up against an unfair law in San Francisco demonstrated that the Bill of Rights belongs to all Americans.

Racial caricatures and stereotyping was a common practice in America during the 19th and 20th centuries.

Lochner v. New York (1905)

Near the turn of the 19th century, the state legislatures had begun responding to the pleas of social reformers and muckrakers. Among them was Upton Sinclair, whose novel *The Jungle,* exposed the deplorable working conditions in the Chicago stockyards. Then, the Supreme Court dealt the cause of working people a serious setback. In *Lochner v. New York*, the Court invalidated a New York law which prohibited bakeries from employing workers for more than 60 hours a week or ten hours a day. The majority found that the statute interfered with the freedom of contract and the 14th Amendment's right to "liberty" guaranteed to both the employer and the employee. Since the law affected only bakers and not the general public, it could not be sustained as a health measure. The Court predicted that if this law were upheld for bakers, other laws could be passed limiting the rights of employers and employees in a host of other businesses. If this happened, the Court reasoned, the right to freely contract the terms and conditions of their employment would be impaired.

In dissent, Justice Oliver Wendell Holmes wrote: "The Constitution is not intended to embody a particular economic theory," by which he no doubt meant "laissez faire." In Holmes' opinion, duly enacted legislation could be upset only if "a rational and fair man necessarily, would admit that the statute proposed would infringe fundamental principles of our people and our law."

Although the Court, twelve years later in *Bunting v. Oregon* (1917), ignored *Lochner* and upheld maximum hour and overtime wage legislation, *Lochner's* theory of "substantive due process" was used for three decades to invalidate economic regulations. It was not until the 1930s that *Lochner* and the doctrine of "substantive due process" fell into disrepute, as the Court began to uphold the constitutionality of pervasive New Deal legislation. Today, given the breadth and depth of state and federal laws regulating almost every facet of working conditions, *Lochner* reflects an almost quaint view in favor of keeping government out of private business matters.

Racist images plagued Chinese Americans.

Chinese Workers labor in the California Goldfields.

When Homer A. Plessy, who was one-eighth black, sat in the "White" car on the East Louisiana Railroad, he was arrested and convicted of violating the law. The Supreme Court held that the object of the 14th Amendment "was undoubtedly to enforce the absolute equality of the two races before the law." In the same breath it added, "but in the nature of things it could not have been intended to abolish distinctions based on color . . ." The lone dissenter, Justice John Marshall Harlan, complained that the decision endorsed segregation which "permits the seeds of race hate to be planted under the sanction of law." Answering the claim of the majority that segregation's "badge of inferiority" exists "solely because the colored race chooses to put that constriction on it," Harlan wrote: "Our Constitution is color-blind, neither knows nor tolerates classes among citizens."

The Court ignored the rights of other minorities as well. In 1887 the Court refused to apply the Civil Rights and Enforcement Acts to the Chinese, and in 1889 upheld a federal ban on Chinese immigration. Likewise, while federal policy patronized American Indians by announcing the goal that "the savage shall become a citizen," the Court, in *Elk v. Wilkins* (1884), held that Indians were not citizens within the meaning of the 14th Amendment.

Meanwhile, the majority of Americans were enjoying an expansion of popular democracy and progressive reform. The work of the progressives inspired the third wave of Constitutional amendments, between 1919 and 1920. They brought about a federal income tax, direct election of senators, prohibition and women's suffrage. At all levels of government there was an increase in the number of administrative agencies, commissions and boards. Congress and the president exercised unprecedented powers, which began to reach into every facet of society and threatened to restrict personal freedoms and individual liberties in ways that often escaped judicial review. A 1918 survey of administrative law warned that "with the great increase of state activity . . . there never was a time" when the value of the Bill of Rights, "will have been so manifest."

But the Supreme Court, under the leadership of Chief Justice William Howard Taft, did not show much interest in the issues of individual rights. Espousing Social Darwinism, the survival of the fittest, the Court's opinions more regularly supported constitutional protection for private property and private enterprise. Between 1921 and 1933, an activist Court struck down 14 acts of Congress, 148 state laws and 12 city ordinances, all because they placed unwarranted governmental restraints on business activity. But the same Court easily upheld federal, state and local laws that helped business, and others restrict the civil liberties of union organizers, radicals, strident pacifists and other critics of capitalism.

While Samuel Gompers, the famous labor leader, would look back on this era and bemoan the fact that "the courts have abolished the Constitution as far as the rights and interests of the working people are concerned," others were convinced that the Court was fulfilling President Coolidge's aphorism that "the business of America is business."

Rosa Parks challenges segregation by sitting in the white section of a bus in 1955.

VOTING RIGHTS FOR WOMEN

Early Woman's Suffrage Convention.

The Bill of Rights was 130 years old before women were guaranteed the right to vote. The women's suffrage movement can be traced to the Seneca Falls Convention in 1848, led by Elizabeth Cady Stanton and Lucretia Mott. The convention resolved "that it is the duty of the women of this country to secure to themselves their sacred right to the elective franchise." Hopes that the coalition of abolitionists and suffragettes would lead to voting rights for *both* women and blacks were dashed when the 15th Amendment, ratified in 1870, only addressed abridgment of the right to vote "on account of race, color or previous condition of servitude."

Arguing that the right to vote in a federal election was a privilege of national citizenship guaranteed by the 14th Amendment, Susan B. Anthony voted in 1872 despite the fact that the New York Constitution limited the franchise to men. She was convicted of casting a ballot in an election for which she was ineligible and fined $100.00. Many of her sister suffragettes went to jail for demonstrations in favor of women's right to vote. In spite of many setbacks, these courageous women won support for a constitutional amendment and planted the seeds for greater rights for women later in the century.

In 1912 Theodore Roosevelt's Progressive Party endorsed women's suffrage and in 1919 Woodrow Wilson announced his support for a constitutional amendment. In 1920, the 19th Amendment, prohibiting denial or abridgment of the right to vote in any election on grounds of sex, was ratified. "The right to vote freely for the candidate of one's choice is of the essence of a democratic society," wrote Chief Justice Earl Warren in 1964, "and any restrictions on that right strike at the heart of representative government."

Susan B. Anthony.

ERA
YES!

Above: Woman's Suffrage Parade, 1915.
Below: Equal Rights Amendment Parade, 1976.

Women reformers arrested by police protecting vice and liquor in 1874 cartoon.

WAR & REACTION

The vitality of America's commitment to freedom of speech is tested, not so much in times of peace and tranquility, but in times of war and external threats, real or imagined. It is one thing to tolerate the other person's offensive ideas when you are safe and secure; it is quite a different matter when you are threatened and at risk. It is in those very times that the First Amendment is most needed and so often abused.

Modern First Amendment law, as articulated by a series of pivotal Supreme Court decisions, was inaugurated during and after World War I. These cases—often in the words of dissenting Justices, not the majorities—represent the birth of our contemporary law of free speech, free press and free assembly.

No case epitomizes the early development of the First Amendment better than *Abrams v. U.S.* In 1918, five Russian Jews were among a group of New York radicals who strenuously opposed U.S. intervention against the Bolshevik Revolution in Russia. Four anarchists and one socialist, they believed the Russian Revolution "would lead to the Int[ernational] Social Revolution and the freeing of mankind."

On August 23, 1918, the five distributed leaflets, printed in English and Yiddish, accusing President Woodrow Wilson of hypocrisy for sending troops into Siberia and exhorting the workers of the world to "awake" and "rise." The more militant of the two circulars urged workers to "spit in the face of the lying, hypocritical, military propaganda." It also warned that "while working in the ammunition factories you are creating bullets, swords, cannons to murder not only Germans, but also your most beloved, your best ones, who are in Russia and who are fighting for freedom."

The five were arrested and charged with violating the federal Sedition Act. Other than writing, printing and circulating the anonymous leaflets, no other overt acts were charged and no adverse consequences to the war effort were alleged.

Protesters against U.S. involvement in World War I.

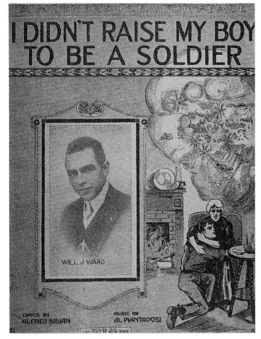

At the height of World War I hysteria, President Wilson had signed the Sedition Act. It made it a crime to "willfully utter, print, write, or publish any disloyal, profane, scurrilous or abusive language" about the United States' form of government, Constitution, military forces, flag or uniform. The Act also forbade the use of any language designed to bring any of these things "into contempt, scorn, contumely or disrepute." The Act also made it illegal for anyone to

> "willfully urge, incite, or advocate any curtailment of production . . . necessary or essential to the prosecution of the war . . . with intent by such curtailment to cripple or hinder the United States in the prosecution of the war."

The Act did not require proof that any such "curtailment" had actually resulted or was even likely to occur.

The conviction of the *Abrams* defendants was a foregone conclusion. In a real sense, they did design the circulars to heap scorn on President Wilson's policy toward Russia and they did urge workers not to make bullets, swords and cannons to kill Russian workers. Thus, the importance of the *Abrams* case is not whether the defendants violated the statute, but whether the statute violated the Constitution.

Anti-war protesters then and now.

BETTER DEAD THAN RED!

Cases and Controversies

Schenck v. United States (1919)

Tested against the government's awesome power during wartime, *Schenck v. United States* was the first U.S. Supreme Court decision interpreting the First Amendment. In it, the Court unanimously upheld the conviction of a Socialist for mailing 15,000 leaflets to draftees. The leaflet quoted the 13th Amendment (abolishing slavery), denounced the draft as unconstitutional and urged young men to "assert their rights" or else be ground into "cannon fodder" to serve the interests of Wall Street. Tried under the 1917 Espionage Act, which made it a federal crime to publish any false statement intended to obstruct the armed forces, Charles Schenck was convicted without any evidence that he had in fact corrupted a single draftee. Writing for a unanimous Court, Justice Holmes held that words could be punished if they "create a clear and present danger." In words oft-repeated (and oft-misquoted) Holmes wrote, "The most stringent protection of free speech would not protect a man in falsely shouting fire in a crowded theater and causing a panic."

Victims of 1920 "Red Raids" at Ellis Island.

Senator McCarthy renews communist scare in 1950.

CHARLOTTE ANITA WHITNEY

Few would have predicted that the niece of Supreme Court Justice Field and the descendant of Mayflower voyagers would emerge in 1919 as a radical social reformer who challenged repressive legislation. Yet, Charlotte Whitney's case set the stage for a historic legal development with Justice Louis Brandeis' germinal defense of the First Amendment. Charlotte Anita Whitney came to believe, first as a Socialist and later as a Communist, that the problems of poverty, hunger and illness would never be solved within the existing political system. As a delegate to the convention of the Communist Labor Party, her call to achieve economic justice through the electoral process was voted down. A more radical policy set by the Industrial Workers of the World (the "Wobblies") was adopted. Still, because of her speech, Whitney was charged with violating the California Criminal Syndicalism Act. Prompted by wartime hysteria, news of the Russian Revolution, rumors of Bolshevik terrorism and widespread labor unrest, the Syndicalism Act made mere speech a crime. Under the Act it became illegal to advocate force and violence to accomplish "a change in industrial ownership or control," or any political change. After a highly publicized trial, Whitney was convicted without any proof that she had engaged or assisted in any violent acts. The Supreme Court upheld her conviction. Because Whitney's lawyers had neglected to raise certain issues, Justices Brandeis and Holmes concurred in that decision. But the poignancy of Justice Brandeis' separate opinion serves to this day as a timeless declaration of the true purpose of free speech and free association. He wrote that those who won our independence believed that:

> "... freedom to think as you will and to speak as you think are means indispensable to the discovery and spread of political truth; that without free speech and assembly discussion would be futile; that with them, discussion affords ordinarily adequate protection against the dissemination of noxious doctrine; that the greatest menace to freedom is an inert people; that public discussion is a political duty; and that this should be a fundamental principle of the American government."

On June 20, 1927, Whitney was pardoned and she spent the rest of her life working for social justice. Fourteen years after her death, in *Brandenburg v. Ohio* (1969), the Supreme Court vindicated Whitney and Brandeis and ruled unanimously that criminal syndicalism laws were unconstitutional.

Communist Headquarters, New York City, circa 1930.

Oliver Wendell Holmes, Jr.

When he retired from the Supreme Court in 1932, after 30 years of service, Justice Oliver Wendell Holmes, Jr., was called "the greatest of our age in the domain of jurisprudence, and one of the greatest of the ages." The son of a famous poet and man of letters, Holmes fought in the Civil War, wrote a comprehensive review of the common law, taught at Harvard Law School and served for 20 years as a Justice of the Massachusetts Supreme Judicial Court. Outside of the area of free speech, Holmes exhibited great deference to the will of the majority as expressed by duly elected legislatures. In this way he became a proponent of "judicial restraint." On the U.S. Supreme Court, particularly in the 1920s, Holmes became known as the "Great Dissenter." Many of his dissents later prevailed as the majority view. But some scholars have concluded that Holmes was "largely indifferent" to civil liberties. They point out that in 1927 he agreed that a state could constitutionally sterilize mental defectives without their consent. "Three generations of imbeciles are enough," he wrote. Throughout a century marked by the expansion of individual rights and a hostility toward unwarranted government interference in private matters, Holmes held back. He developed a jurisprudence which one scholar characterized as standing for the proposition "that the state, as agent of the majority, can do what it likes until some other majority seizes power." Perhaps more than his specific rulings, Holmes is honored for elevating the literature of judicial decision. His high intellect, unique style and his unflinching capacity to engage his readers' emotions, guarantee him a place among the most influential Justices to have served on the Supreme Court.

Oliver Wendell Holmes, 1902.

Patriotic appeals from World War I.

A young Oliver Wendell Holmes on cover of *Vanity Fair*, 1862.

This Is An Am-er-ican Boy.
What Did He Do?
He Gave His Life For His
Count-ry.
If He Was Wil-ling To Give
His Life, Aren't You Wil-ling
To Lend Your Mon-ey?

By the time the *Abrams* case reached the U.S. Supreme Court, Justice Oliver Wendell Holmes, Jr., already had begun to tackle the knotty question of reconciling freedom of expression with national security. In March of 1919, Holmes wrote for a unanimous Court upholding three convictions under the Espionage Act in the *Schenck, Frohwerk* and *Debs* decisions. Based on a leaflet, newspaper articles and a speech, respectively, Holmes found that words which "create a clear and present danger that they will bring about the substantive evils that Congress has a right to prevent" can be punished without violating the First Amendment. In perhaps his most memorable phrase, Holmes wrote that the First Amendment did not prevent one from being punished for "falsely shouting fire in a crowded theater and causing a panic."

But between those decisions in March and the *Abrams* decision on November 10, 1919, Holmes' views changed. He had gained a new sensitivity to the values of free speech, to the importance of experimentation and to the need to treat dissenters mercifully.

When the *Abrams* decision was announced, the unbroken line of *unanimous* opinions upholding convictions for seditious speech ended. Holmes dissented and Justice Louis Brandeis joined him. Holmes wrote that "the best test of truth is the power of the thought to get itself accepted in the competition of the market."

Holmes' "clear and present danger" test, which had sealed the three prior convictions, now, in his dissent, became the "clear and imminent danger" test—a shield to protect free speech. Congress could constitutionally punish speech only if it actually presented an "imminent . . . danger of immediate evil." Holmes found no such danger from the "silly leaflet" in *Abrams*. In essence, regardless of whether the *Abrams* defendants had falsely shouted fire in a theater, they had not caused a panic.

In time, the repression of controversial political speech, suffered by opponents of the United States' role in World War I and by proponents of alternative economic and political systems, would become the exception, rather than the rule. To be sure, America would experience another "Red Scare" and other episodes of intolerance. But the lessons of this era, taught in the words of Holmes and Brandeis, would serve the Bill of Rights well, as precedents on which to build more widespread acceptance of the value of dissent in a democratic society.

The United States
Supreme Court, 1916.

CHAPTER 9

FROM NORMALCY TO THE GREAT DEPRESSION

"When Shall We Three Meet Again?"

1920s cartoon inspired by Scope's Trial which debated teaching of evolution.

American participation in World War I in 1917-18 had enormous effects upon the fabric of life in the United States. This "Great War" marked the emergence of America as a major world power and changed the course of our legal history, particularly in areas involving the Bill of Rights. Widespread fears of dissent, especially emerging from the Russian Revolution, provoked powerful governmental attacks on civil liberties. The "Red Scare" of 1919-1920 combined restrictive federal and state legislation and Supreme Court decisions to chill political dissent and free expression.

As the nation moved from wartime to peace in the 1920s, American life became more colorful and complex. The 1920s in the United States had no central event like a war to define its basic character. Popularly known as "The Jazz Age," the 20s highlighted Prohibition; illegal liquor distribution and consumption; gangsters; and radically new developments in music, dance, literature, and personal fashion. For many people, it was a time of "normalcy," in striking contrast to the wartime environment of only a few years earlier.

Above all, widespread economic prosperity caused a dramatic rise in the standard of living for millions of Americans. Cars, appliances, and new recreational opportunities such as radio and the movies enhanced their quality of life. The elections of Warren Harding, Calvin Coolidge

Federal agent destroy illegal alcohol.

Temperance art show the benefits of taking pledge against drinking alcohol.

and Herbert Hoover during this era reflected widespread satisfaction with social and economic developments and priorities in America. Despite the impending catastrophe of the Depression, most Americans appeared happier than at any time in the recent past.

This reaction to "normalcy," however, was not universal. Large pockets of poverty remained, especially among urban and rural racial minorities, farmers, and industrial workers. Ku Klux Klan activity increased dramatically, bringing terror and violence to thousands of victims, mostly African Americans. Labor unrest and strife also spread throughout the United States, fostered by low wages and poor working conditions, strong employer resistance to union organizing, and several anti-labor legal decisions in the Federal Courts.

Other legal changes during the 20s had powerful implications for the Bill of Rights. A key development was a decision by the United States Supreme Court in 1925. In *Gitlow v. New York,* the Court took the momentous step of ruling that the word "liberty" in the due process clause of the 14th Amendment of the Constitution includes liberty of speech as guaranteed by the First Amendment. Known as the incorporation doctrine, this meant that the same restrictions applying to the Federal Government in the First Amendment also apply to state and local governments. After *Gitlow* the same rights that people had regarding freedom of religion, of speech, of the press, of petition, and of assembly in the national arena would now apply everywhere. A person could now speak or worship freely without interference from *any* level of government—all resulting from the Supreme Court's bold use of the 14th Amendment.

Deeper social, economic, and political realities also affected the Constitutional rights of American citizens and other residents. The post-war prosperity of the 1920s turned quickly into unprecedented economic disaster, making life desperate for millions of Americans. Catalyzed by the great stock market crash of 1929, a devastating combination of institutional and natural calamities changed the social, political, and legal landscape of life in the United States. The tumultuous events of the 1930s are vital in understanding both the effectiveness and limitations of the Bill of Rights in actual practice.

In 1933, at the time of the first inauguration of President Franklin Delano Roosevelt, 25 percent of the American labor force was out of work. In the President's words, "one-third of a nation" was "ill-housed, ill-clad, and ill-nourished" — a far cry from the "pockets of poverty" of the 1920s. The grim pattern of urban bread lines and the resulting human despair became the hallmark of life during the Great Depression. To add to the tragedy, once-fertile land turned into dustbowls, with all the accompanying human suffering described by John Steinbeck in *The Grapes of Wrath.*

"Flappers" of the Jazz Age.

That memorable novel, like the equally classic documentary photographs produced under the authority of the Farm Security Administration, chronicled the human tragedy of uprooted, impoverished Americans moving westward from Oklahoma, Arkansas, and several other states. Agricultural decline and economic stagnation forced these "Oakies" and "Arkies" to migrate elsewhere, especially to California, to seek subsistence wages as migrant field laborers.

Labor Protests at Republic Steel, 1937.

Benjamin Gitlow, 1928.

Cases and Controversies

Gitlow v. New York (1925)

In 1925, New York radical agitator Benjamin Gitlow published a pamphlet entitled "The Left Wing Manifesto." Like many communist writings of the era, this essay was full of inflammatory rhetoric encouraging workers to organize strikes and revolutionary actions to overthrow the capitalist economy and government. Gitlow was thoroughly direct in his appeal: "The proletariat revolution and communist reconstruction of society . . . is now indispensable . . . The Communist International calls the proletariat of the world to the final struggle!"

Not surprisingly, the authorities responded harshly to such revolutionary prose. Gitlow was swiftly indicted and convicted for violating the New York criminal anarchy statute. In his appeal to the U.S. Supreme Court, he claimed that this law was unconstitutional because it violated his right to freedom of expression under the First Amendment. Gitlow's lawyers asked the Court to ignore a major legal precedent and rule that the First Amendment applied to the states as well as to the Federal Government. In 1833, the Supreme Court had ruled in *Barron v. Baltimore* that the Bill of Rights only protected citizens from actions of the Federal Government. Under this decision, the free expression rights of the First Amendment restrained only Congress and other agencies of the National Government. States like New York were free to regulate or even ban political speeches and publications, including the revolutionary efforts of Mr. Gitlow.

Walter Pollak, one of Gitlow's lawyers, used an imaginative legal argument for his client. Instead of attacking the *Barron* decision directly, he maintained that the 14th Amendment was the truly applicable provision of the Constitution in this case. He claimed that the language of that Amendment, which says "nor shall any State deprive any person of life, liberty, or property, without due process of law," included liberty of the press as guaranteed in the First Amendment. The basic point, therefore, was that no state could deprive a person of freedom of expression without violating the 14th Amendment.

Pollak was obviously persuasive. Justice Edward Sanford's ruling for the Court established the incorporation doctrine that fundamentally expanded the rights of free expression to restrain *all* governmental bodies throughout the United States: "For present purposes we may and do assume that freedom of speech and of the press—which are protected by the First Amendment from abridgement by Congress—are among the fundamental personal rights and 'liberties' protected by the due process clause of the 14th Amendment from impairment by the states."

This extraordinary expansion of freedom of the press, ironically, did nothing for Benjamin Gitlow himself, at least not immediately. The Supreme Court held that New York had *not* violated Gitlow's First and Fourteenth Amendment rights because "The Left Wing Manifesto" was not mere philosophical expression, but rather "direct incitement." The Court upheld his criminal conviction on this ground.

After serving time in prison, Gitlow continued his radical political activity. Much later in his life, he turned from his past and became a leading spokesperson for right-wing movements. Some of his later writings were equally inflammatory, distributed nationally by extremist organizations like the Christian Crusade and the John Birch Society. These provocative political expressions, however, caused no legal problems for their author. The 1925 decision of *Gitlow v. New York* ensured that they were fully protected by the First Amendment.

Left-wing propaganda magazine of the 1930s.

NRA MEMBER U.S.
WE DO OUR PART

President Asks Fifteen-Judge Supreme Court in Shake-up

A modern equivalent
of the Dust Bowl:
today's homeless.

Dust Bowl refugees
take to the road.

NEXT TIME TRY THE TRAIN
RELAX Southern Pacific

EMMA GOLDMAN BEFORE HER JUDGES
"If giving one's life for the purpose of awakening social conscious-
ness in the masses, a consciousness which will impel them to bring quality
and not quantity in society, be a crime, I am glad to be such a criminal."

MOTHER EARTH

Vol. XI.   May, 1916   No. 3

MAY DAY

Migrant work was harsh and the pay was minimal. Equally tragic was the human reaction to these migrant families. Frequently cursed and ill-treated on their trek westward, they also encountered legal barriers totally prohibited by the Constitution. Many "Oakies" were turned back by state and local police authorities at the California state line. Informed bluntly that there was no room for people without adequate funds, they were often denied the right to travel guaranteed by the privileges and immunities clause of Section 2 of Article IV of the Constitution and fortified by the Ninth and Fourteenth amendments.

To compound American domestic troubles, the labor unrest of the 1920s intensified during the following decade. Organized labor had been suppressed for many decades. Under Roosevelt's New Deal Administration, however, laws like the Wagner Act helped unions to obtain recognition from large corporations. This legislation added to the more basic rights of working people to organize, assemble, and seek redress of their grievances by exercising their First Amendment rights.

The struggle to fully implement these rights was not without violence on both sides. Bloodshed was commonplace and police were often employed in the interests of management. Professional strike breakers were used to defeat the organizing efforts of many labor unions. Striking workers abused strike breakers and sabotaged factories. One horrific incident took place on Memorial Day, 1937. About a thousand workers at the Republic Steel Company in Gary, Indiana and their families attended a rally, where they planned a protest march to the plant, a short distance away. They never reached their destination because the police charged the crowd with tear gas, clubs, and bullets, killing several marchers.

The Great Depression era also generated significant legal developments. The New Deal Administration had been regularly frustrated during the 1930s when many of its key economic and social legislative acts were declared invalid by a more conservative Supreme Court. In response, Roosevelt sought to reorganize the Court by adding as many as six new members. This "court-packing" plan failed. Yet, the political pressure from the White House succeeded in modifying the Court's hostility to New Deal reforms. By the end of the decade, Roosevelt had filled several vacancies on the Court with justices more sympathetic to his programs.

In 1937, the Supreme Court also extended the incorporation doctrine. In *Palko v. Connecticut*, the Court held that the due process clause of the 14th Amendment prohibits states from depriving people of rights "implicit in the concept of ordered liberty." The case required the selective incorporation of the Bill of Rights into the 14th Amendment. The practical effect of this decision has been the absorption into the due process clause of almost all the provisions of the Bill of Rights. Following the rationale of the *Palko* case, the major protections of the Bill of Rights are now fully applicable to state and local governments.

Police and strikers clash in 1937.

Margaret Sanger
(1879-1966)

Mrs. Margaret Sanger.

argaret Sanger testi-
s before Congress.

Trained as a nurse, Margaret Sanger began working in the slums of New York City in 1912. She quickly discovered that the poor health and misery of slum mothers were frequently caused by constant child bearing or illegal abortions, sometimes self-induced. Sanger later wrote about the case of a 28-year-old mother of three young children who tried to end her own pregnancy using an instrument borrowed from a neighbor. A doctor and Sanger saved the young woman's life, but when she pleaded for "the secret" to prevent future pregnancies, the doctor said he could do nothing to help her. At this time, it was against the law for even doctors to provide information about contraception. Three months later, the young woman was dead after another attempt at a self-administered abortion.

Sanger decided to abandon her nursing career and became a crusader for the freedom of women to choose whether to become a mother and how many children to have. Sanger coined the term,"birth control," and, in 1914, wrote a pamphlet describing different contraceptive methods. In 1916, she and her sister opened the nation's first birth control clinic in a poor section of Brooklyn. A few days after the clinic opened, Sanger was arrested and then convicted for illegally distributing contraception literature. She was sentenced to a month in jail. The New York Court of Appeals upheld her conviction, but it also ruled that physicians could legally prescribe contraceptives.

Following World War I, at a time when Americans were attempting to "return to normalcy," Sanger challenged American morality by stepping up her efforts to spread information about contraceptive devices and methods. "No woman can call herself free who does not own and control her own body," she wrote in 1920.

After the Second World War, Sanger helped to found the International Planned Parenthood Federation. She also raised funds for research into more effective birth control methods. This effort finally led to the development of "the pill" in the 1950s. She also continued her campaign against anti-contraception laws. One year before Sanger died, the U.S. Supreme Court ruled that state laws forbidding the sale of birth control devices to married persons violated their right to privacy and were unconstitutional *(Griswold v. Connecticut,* 1965). Margaret Sanger had inspired a change in what is protected under the Bill of Rights.

choice

Pro and anti-abortion advocates in confrontation, 1986.

75

Los Angeles Times

ALL THE NEWS ALL THE TIME

LARGEST HOME-DELIVERED CIRCULATION
LARGEST ADVERTISING VOLUME

M.A.dison 2345
The Times Telephone Number

LIBERTY UNDER THE LAW   TRUE INDUSTRIAL FREEDOM

IN THREE PARTS — 42 PAGES

TIMES OFFICE

VOL. LXI   CCC   MONDAY MORNING, DECEMBER 8, 1941.   DAILY, FIVE CENTS

JAPS OPEN WAR ON U.S. WITH BOMBING OF HAWAII

Japanese Americans
Relocation Order
Poster, 1942.

Poster urging increased war
production on the homefront
during World War II.

GIVE 'EM BOTH BARRELS

WESTERN DEFENSE COMMAND AND FOURTH ARMY
WARTIME CIVIL CONTROL ADMINISTRATION
Presidio of San Francisco, California
May 10, 1942

INSTRUCTIONS TO ALL PERSONS OF JAPANESE ANCESTRY

Living in the Following Area:

THE SECOND WORLD WAR

Nothing in human history is comparable to the Second World War. From 1939 to 1945, the war killed more people, disrupted more lives, and had more profound emotional, economic, political and social consequences than any other war in history. The Allied battle against the Axis powers of Germany, Italy and Japan also had enormous implications for domestic life in the United States.

The U.S. had been committed psychologically, politically and economically to the Allied cause ever since the Nazi invasion of Poland in 1939. Formal American involvement in the Second World War began after the Japanese bombing of Pearl Harbor, Hawaii on December 7, 1941. The war brought a resurgence of optimism to an American public still ravaged by the massive economic hardships of the Great Depression of the 1930s. Military spending and industrial mobilization for the war effort provided the nation's economy with the boost it needed for full recovery.

The new economic optimism was tempered by a powerful fear of a Japanese invasion of the U.S. mainland. The military and many Americans saw Pearl Harbor as merely the first of several potential targets. Residents of California, Oregon and Washington in particular saw their own communities in imminent danger. Widespread public fear soon transformed itself into attacks on fellow citizens and resident aliens of Japanese ancestry. Fueled by persistent but unproved rumors that the Japanese-American community contained spies and saboteurs, the press began a campaign to demand their evacuation.

Fearful Americans were prepared to believe anything, despite the absence of evidence: that Japanese-American domestics were gathering intelligence information for transmittal to Tokyo and that Japanese-American farmers were hoarding food supplies to feed an invading Imperial army. Hostile signs and violent incidents against Japanese-Americans became increasingly common in the early months of 1942. Faced with growing political and military pressure, President Franklin Roosevelt proclaimed Executive Order 9066 on February 19, allowing military commanders to designate areas "from

Japanese American family finds house vandalized when they return home.

WPA Poster.

Minoru Yasui

Ordered evacuated in 1942 from their homes and relocated to desolate camps, most Japanese-Americans saw few alternatives to complying. Reluctantly, they settled their affairs, sold whatever property they could, gathered the few possessions permitted, and reported for transportation to temporary detention centers. They endured the emotional stress of confinement and the humiliation of being regarded as traitors and spies.

Some resisted the order to relocate. Men like Gordon Hirabayashi, Fred Korematsu, Minoru Yasui and others refused to obey, suffering arrest and imprisonment for their courageous conduct. Yasui had seen enough discrimination against Japanese-Americans all of his life. As a boy, he watched his father forced to abandon his dream of becoming a lawyer because he was unable, as an Asian, to obtain American citizenship. Yasui resolved to fight.

Becoming a lawyer himself, Yasui knew well how his *nisei* friends, second generation Japanese-Americans, suffered discrimination in jobs and housing. Following Pearl Harbor, he tried to serve in the United States Army, where he held a commission as a reserve officer. He was informed that he was unacceptable for service.

The military curfew order for persons of Japanese ancestry infuriated him. He believed the order violated the Constitution. Testing the curfew, he notified the military of his refusal to obey. Inevitably, he soon landed in jail. Shortly after posting bail, the military issued the evacuation order. Again, Yasui refused to comply. Within the week he was arrested by military police. Soon he was on his way to the temporary detention facilities in Portland where other Japanese-Americans from Oregon were sent. Then he was sent on to a camp in rural Idaho.

Returned under guard to Portland, he was convicted of the original curfew violation. His expedited appeal to the U.S. Supreme Court failed, and he and Hirabayashi's convictions were upheld when the Court sustained the curfew order. As a result, he served nine months in jail before being returned to the Idaho internment camp. While there, he continued to protest the unjust incarceration of his people.

Years later, Yasui continues to feel angry about the events of 1942 to 1945. Even though his own conviction has been vacated, he sees the experience in broader historical terms: "This should never be done to anyone else, but the sad thing is that it could happen again. Unless we are all vigilant to protect the rights of others, it can happen to us."

Japanese Americans being searched after being caught in raid in Los Angeles.

Japanese Americans clear land for planting at Manzanar Relocation Camp, California.

The Mochida family ready for evacuation.

which any or all persons may be excluded." Under this order, 110,000 Japanese and Americans of Japanese descent were removed from their homes and jobs in the Pacific Coast states and interned in remote camps scattered throughout the western and southern United States.

The relocation proceeded without major public opposition. The legal issues were decided in 1944 by the Supreme Court in *Korematsu v. United States*. This case upheld the exclusion order by declaring that it was within the Constitution's war power for the military to conclude that the presence of the Japanese-Americans constituted a present or potential danger to American security. Dissenting Justices Owen Roberts, Frank Murphy and Robert Jackson maintained that the relocation was unconstitutional. They cited the constitutional mandate that the writ of habeas corpus shall not be suspended and the Fifth Amendment guarantee of due process of law.

The deeper roots of this internment of 110,000 people lie in a century of anti-Asian attitudes and actions in America preceding Executive Order 9066. Nativist sentiments, racist legislation and legal decisions, and overtly violent acts against Japanese-Americans long before Pearl Harbor provided the broader context of public fear. For some, the attack on Pearl Harbor was a convenient pretext to make enormous profits from Japanese-Americans forced to liquidate their property and possessions at prices far below market value. In spite of these hardships, thousands of Japanese-Americans served with distinction in the U.S. armed services during the war.

Wartime fears in the early 1940s generated other, less well-known examples of political measures infringing the fundamental values of the Bill of Rights. The imposition of martial law and the suspension of constitutional rights in the Territory of Hawaii from 1941 to 1944 was one of the most glaring. Imposed in the original fear of immediate invasion by Japan, military control of Hawaii began only a few hours after the attack on Pearl Harbor. The territorial governor and the military commander announced that civilian courts were closed and that all governmental functions were placed under the Army's control. The military regime assumed total political and administrative power over Hawaii's population of 465,000 people.

Persons suspected of disloyalty, mostly of Japanese descent, were rounded up and imprisoned. The Army decreed compulsory fingerprinting, maintained strict censorship on the press, broadcasting and the civilian mails, instituted a rigorous curfew, and enforced blackout orders keeping civilian homes darkened after sunset. Military control, in short, was total. It lasted throughout the war, long after the fear of imminent invasion had passed.

Serious criminal cases were conducted by military tribunals rather than civil courts. Trials were judged by military officers without juries. Written charges were not furnished to criminal defendants and arrests, searches and seizures of evidence were made without warrants. Trials in Honolulu lasted about five minutes each, with guilty verdicts in more than 99% of the cases.

Japanese Here Begin Exodus

Nation's Greatest Mass Evacuation Starts as Vanguard of 35,000 Southland Nipponese Moves to Owens Valley Concentration Center

79

Fred Korematsu, Minoru Yasui, and Gordon Hirabayashi file papers to have their cases re-opened in 1983.

Korematsu v. United States (1944)

The evacuation and imprisonment of more than 110,000 Japanese-Americans in 1942 is widely regarded as one of the darkest moments in our constitutional history. Yet, the United States Supreme Court upheld the internment in its 1944 decision in *Korematsu v. United States*. Executive Order 9066 called for three measures in officially designated military areas: (1) persons of Japanese descent were placed under curfew from 8:00 P.M. until 6:00 A.M.; (2) they could be excluded from these areas by a military order; and (3) they would be relocated to internment camps until their loyalty to the United States could be determined.

Each part of the order raised major constitutional issues and were resolved in separate decisions of the Supreme Court. Its first ruling, *Hirabayashi v. United States,* upheld the criminal curfew conviction of a Japanese-American who disobeyed both the curfew and the exclusion orders. The Court declined to consider the more serious issue of the exclusion order.

More than a year later, in December, 1944, the Court ruled on the other parts of the evacuation program. In *Korematsu,* the Court found no constitutional barrier to excluding an American citizen of Japanese descent from his home town in California. In a companion case decided the same day, *Ex Parte Endo,* the Court avoided a constitutional decision on the internment itself. It merely noted that prolonged detention was not authorized.

The rationale of all three Japanese-American cases reveals how the Supreme Court bowed to the overwhelming military and political pressures of wartime fears. Above all, it refused to examine the factual basis for the military's judgment that Japanese-Americans were security risks threatening national security. Ignoring the fact that no Japanese-Americans had committed any espionage or sabotage since Pearl Harbor, the Court noted that it "cannot say" that the military determination was wrong.

Justice Frank Murphy, dissenting in *Korematsu,* strongly attacked the military for making wholesale judgments based on racial stereotypes. Justices Robert Jackson and Owen Roberts also found the majority's opinion constitutionally flawed. Many years later, political scientist and lawyer Peter Irons discovered definitive evidence that the government deliberately misled the Court on issues about the military necessity of the evacuation. Following his revelations, federal courts in the mid-1980s set aside the criminal convictions of Gordon Hirabayashi, his co-defendant Minoru Yasui, and Fred Korematsu. The United States Congress also provided reparation payments to survivors of the internment camps. Legally, justice finally prevailed. Historically, the Japanese Exclusion stands as a dark chapter in our past when the Bill of Rights failed to protect individual rights.

Japanese American troops of the 100th Infantry Battalion in Italy, 1944.

ZOOT SUIT

A New American Play by **LUIS VALDEZ**
August 17-October 1 Mark Taper Forum
Gordon Davidson Artistic Director · Center Theatre Group · Music Center ✪
World Premiere First Production of the 1978-79 Season

Illustration by Ignacio Gomez for the World Premiere of "Zoot Suits" by Luis Valdez at the Mark Taper Forum.

Prisoners convicted under martial law tribunals sought legal relief from the Federal Courts. Finally, in February, 1946—five months after the Japanese surrender ended World War II—the U.S. Supreme Court in the companion cases of *Duncan v. Kahanamoku* and *White v. Steer* declared that the trial of civilians by military courts had been without legal authority. This judicial declaration from the highest court in the land reaffirmed the principle that constitutional rights are as important in times of war as in times of peace.

Wartime hysteria affected other civilian groups in the United States during the early 1940s. Women and ethnic minorities found increased economic opportunities resulting from military needs and intensified production requirements. Still, the deeper anxieties of wartime increased the long history of racial tension in the United States. The atmosphere in Los Angeles, for example, was tense and volatile, particularly against the Chicano community.

In 1942, the press promoted fears of Mexican crime, focusing especially on young Mexican-American men wearing "zoot suits," long jackets and trousers flared at the knees and tight at the ankles. The Los Angeles City Council passed an ordinance that prohibited the wearing of zoot suits and police roamed throughout Mexican-American areas making searches and terrorizing the population. In August, 1942, a young Mexican was found near death on a dirt road near the Sleepy Lagoon just outside the city. After his death, the police rounded up 22 gang members and beat confessions out of them. Several were convicted of murder and other serious criminal charges. Fortunately, this miscarriage of justice was later reversed.

A similar episode occurred the following year in Los Angeles, when soldiers and sailors, who took the zoot suit as a sign of disloyalty, stormed into bars and other establishments. They beat young Chicanos, tearing the zoot suits from their bodies. Civilian and military police did not stop the rampage, and even arrested young Mexican-Americans on baseless charges. The local press meanwhile intensified the hysteria. The riot eventually ended, but the long term consequences affected Southern California for decades to come.

The Second World War ended in a total military victory against the fascist powers of Europe and Asia. It signified a remarkable accomplishment for a unified America capable of mobilizing enormous resources in a common struggle against totalitarian forces. At the same time, the experience of the war, with all its attendant fears and anxieties, revealed again that constitutions and laws are not enough in themselves to ensure domestic liberty. The experiences of the Japanese-American internees, the civilian residents of Hawaii and the Mexican-American youth of Los Angeles illustrate the continuing tension between the ideals of the Bill of Rights, especially in times of political stress and military emergency.

World War II victory celebration in New York City.

Mexican-American teenagers celebrate end of Zoot Suit hostilities in Los Angeles, 1943.

THE COLD WAR

When the United States dropped atomic bombs on the Japanese cities of Hiroshima and Nagasaki on August 6 and August 9, 1945, the Second World War ended and a new world began. The nuclear age altered forever the political relationships among nations and began several decades of confrontation between the superpower nations of America and the Soviet Union. This reality of world politics would dominate the second half of the 20th century, affecting not only international relationships, but also domestic life in the United States.

The conflict between the U.S. and the Soviet Union, brewing even before the end of World War II, intensified quickly after the defeat of the Axis powers. Under dictator Josef Stalin, the Soviet Union brutally secured control over most of Eastern Europe. Soviet domination of the region through military conquest and political subversion generated powerful counter measures by the United States and its Western European allies. In March, 1947, U.S. President Harry Truman announced the Truman Doctrine. With it, the United States sought to contain Soviet expansion by providing for American economic and military resources to resist Soviet advances in Greece, Turkey and elsewhere in Europe.

This opening phase of the Cold War led to a set of complex American responses to Soviet power in the final years of the 1940s:

the Marshall Plan, the North Atlantic Treaty Organization (NATO), and the Berlin airlift. Then in September of 1949, the Soviets exploded their own atomic bomb, three years earlier than expected. In February 1950 the British revealed that a scientist who worked on the American atomic bomb had turned over valuable secrets to the Soviets. These events both fostered and intensified widespread public fear in America about a potential nuclear war with the Soviet Union. The press ran stories on the dangers of Soviet power and focused attention on internal threats of communist infiltration and subversion. Rumors of communist spies abounded, compounded by actual revelations of Soviet espionage activities in Europe and the United States. Alger Hiss, a former official of the State Department, was accused of being a member of the Communist party and a spy for the Soviets. Eventually, he was convicted of perjury. Communists Julius and Ethel Rosenberg were accused of supplying atomic bomb secrets to the Soviet Union. Convicted of conspiracy to commit espionage, they were executed in 1953. Both the Hiss and Rosenberg cases were very controversial at the time and are debated even today.

The reactions in America might be compared to those immediately after the 1941 Pearl Harbor attack, when concern about Japanese invasion and subversion developed into public hysteria. Anxiety about Soviet political and military powers was well-founded. Many also sincerely believed that America was in danger. It is debateable, however, whether the genuine dangers of internal communist infiltration justified the degree of legislative and executive actions taken to ensure loyalty and restrict First Amendment guarantees of association, press and speech, and Fifth Amendment protections against self-incrimination.

President Truman initiated a series of internal policies that intensified throughout the 1950s. Loyalty programs, the Attorney General's list of subversive organizations, and criminal indictments of American Communist leaders generated a climate of fear throughout the United States. Many

people worried about their past political associations, including youthful efforts during the Depression that might be construed as sympathetic to communism.

Some sought to dispel suspicion by denouncing present and former friends and colleagues. Loyalty oaths were required in schools, colleges, government agencies, and even private companies. The FBI increased surveillance of real and imagined political radicals. Immigration officials subjected aging immigrants with "suspect" backgrounds to harassment and even deportation. Hundreds of prominent artists, intellectuals and political dissenters had their passports withdrawn, effectively denying them the right to travel abroad for political expression, economic survival, or any other reason.

This pattern of political repression continued in several other forms. The House Un-American Activities Committee and Senate Internal Security Subcommittee regularly summoned people, particularly in the arts and entertainment communities, to explain their political beliefs and identify others who might be Communists. Many state legislatures created their own versions of these federal investigating entities, with little regard for constitutional guarantees of free expression, due process of law, and freedom from self-incrimination. Those asserting their right to remain silent were dubbed "Fifth Amendment Communists." They could be subjected to dismissal from jobs, negative publicity and severe public ostracism. People lost their livelihoods because of past or present political beliefs and associations. Blacklists became a factor in employment, most powerfully in the Hollywood film and television industry. Some who defied the investigating committees were indicted for contempt of Congress and served periods of imprisonment.

UNITED NATIONS ... SORT OF

Senator Joseph R. McCarthy

Joseph McCarthy and his aides.

Joseph R. McCarthy, U.S. Senator from Wisconsin from 1947 to 1957, was a central figure during the wave of political repression in the early Cold War era. His effectiveness in making dramatic but groundless charges of communist subversion against individuals, groups and institutions elevated him to center stage for several years, resulting from his skill in manipulating the media.

As a young man, McCarthy practiced law in Wisconsin, soon gaining election as a circuit judge. During World War II, he served with the Marines, earning the rank of captain. In 1946, he won the race for the U.S. Senate in Wisconsin. His early years there were obscure.

McCarthy's rise to national prominence began with a speech on February 9, 1950, in Wheeling, West Virginia. He claimed that he had in his hand a list of 205 communists serving in the Federal Government. He repeated his allegations, capturing national attention for the next four years. Trading on his war record and tough talk, won him enormous popularity in a nation wracked with fears of Soviet power and internal subversion.

Challenged to produce evidence of his charges, McCarthy refused. Instead, he produced new allegations for radio and television. When he became Chairman of the Senate Permanent Investigations Subcommittee in 1953, he used unidentified informers and made more unfounded accusations, ruining lives and careers in the process.

In 1954, he accused the Secretary of the Army of trying to conceal evidence of espionage that McCarthy had uncovered at Fort Monmouth, New Jersey. The Army in turn accused the Senator of improper conduct by trying to gain favorable treatment for an Army private, a former consultant to his senate subcommittee. Lengthy televised hearings on the charges relating to the Army followed. McCarthy's performance had exposed his true character to the general public. Like many of his fellow Senators, millions of Americans, including his supporters, finally saw McCarthy in action, bullying witnesses and making snide attacks. In a very dramatic moment, McCarthy found himself confronted by mild-mannered Joseph Welsh, the Army's attorney. A hush followed, then the audience burst into applause.

By December, 1954, the Senate voted to "condemn" him because of his questionable finances, his abusive conduct, and his insults to the Senate itself. This effectively ended his public career. His Senatorial and national influence diminished until his death in 1957. For all his notoriety, Joseph McCarthy was largely an opportunist, whose crusade lacked substance. Yet, his methods and early successes stand as a warning that the Bill of Rights can be endangered even in America.

Hollywood writers go on trial for contempt of Congress, 1950.

Not all Americans supported the governmental actions. As early as 1952, a series of protests called for an end to the investigations. In addition, a number of Hollywood stars went to Washington to denounce the accusations against fellow actors.

Senator Joseph R. McCarthy of Wisconsin was a relatively late entry into the "witch hunting" zeal of the 1950s. An opportunist, he seized on the mounting fear to advance his own political career. His unique gift for manipulating the media, through groundless but effective charges of communist subversion, enabled him to occupy center stage for several years. His activities came to provide the label of "McCarthyism," the tactic of publicizing disloyalty or subversion with little evidence.

The pervasive fear of those times had an impact on the intellectual and cultural life of the nation. Books and magazines were removed from stores and libraries and even personal collections in private homes. Foreign mail was carefully scrutinized for subversive influences. Books, paintings and films by writers and artists with left-wing associations became suspect. Financing and distribution of controversial materials became difficult, driving many creative people from their lifelong work in public communication. Teachers at all educational levels became cautious about their classroom comments and private discourse. In short, a powerful chill on the free expression of ideas hovered over the political landscape.

Throughout this era of McCarthyism, the Supreme Court had ample opportunity to define citizens' rights under various provisions of the Bill of Rights. Some of the Court's decisions upheld the rights of citizens to speak freely, to associate with people of their own choice, and to be afforded proper procedures in defending themselves against allegations of subversion. Other decisions by the high court held that the government's interest in self-preservation outweighed individual rights of free expression and political dissent.

The ambivalence of the Supreme Court during this era was reflected in two major decisions about the constitutionality of the Smith Act, which made it a criminal offense to advocate the violent overthrow of the government. In 1951, the Court held in *Dennis v. United States* that this legislation violated no provision of the First Amendment. In 1957, however, the Court held in *Yates v. United States* that the Smith Act did not forbid advocacy and teaching of forcible overthrow as an abstract principle, except "where such advocacy is directed to inciting or producing imminent lawless action and is likely to incite or produce such action."

Eventually, the decisions of the Supreme Court and public opinion re-affirmed the doctrines of the Bill of Rights. Joseph McCarthy was discredited and died in near obscurity. The House Un-American Activities Committee was disbanded.

Most Americans came to regard the tactics and consequences of the era as a tragic injustice. Yet it still stands out as a time like those of the Alien and Sedition Acts, the "Red Scare" following World War I, and the unfair treatment of the Japanese during the Second World War, that tested America's values as expressed in the Bill of Rights.

Students protest
against McCarthy hearings.

Paul Robeson

Paul Robeson was one of the most talented persons of his era. An accomplished athlete, actor, concert singer, orator, musicologist, and political and civil rights activist, his achievements were legendary. He was one of the first African Americans to become an All-American in college football and was a star in college baseball, basketball and track. He was the third black to graduate from Columbia Law School and among the first major black film stars to become internationally famous. As a stage actor he gave a memorable performance of Shakespeare's *Othello* and became one of America's finest concert artists. He spoke more than 20 languages, including Chinese and Russian. As a political figure he worked for African and African American liberation. His achievements spanned a lifetime from the early 20th century to his death in 1976.

Equally remarkable, comparatively few Americans in the 1990s have ever heard of Paul Robeson. The major reason is that he was one of the most prominent of the thousands of victims of McCarthyism. Highly sympathetic to the Soviet Union and a believer in communist ideals, Robeson was effectively black listed during the 1950s. Openly and proudly radical, he enraged his accusers. As a result, he was unable to earn a living despite his international fame. Owners of concert halls and recording studios succumbed to pressure to deny him performances. Record stores refused to carry his recordings, cutting off his royalty income. The FBI followed him to meetings, performances in black churches, and home.

Like hundreds of other artists, he was called to testify before the House Un-American Activities Committee, where his defiant refusal to cooperate only provoked more trouble. In 1950, the State Department cancelled his passport on the grounds that his travels abroad were not in America's best interest. Exiled in his own land, Robeson lost the right to perform overseas, his only remaining source of income. He filed suit to regain his passport. In 1958, after eight years, the Supreme Court in the case of *Kent v. Dulles* ruled that the Secretary of State did not have the right to deny a passport because of a person's alleged communist beliefs or associates. Beyond the value of this legal victory to himself, Robeson's passport struggle helped to establish the right of all Americans to travel abroad.

His passport restored, Robeson resumed his artistic career. He gave concerts throughout the world and once again performed *Othello* in England. He continued to speak critically about American domestic and international policies. But he never truly recovered from his ordeal with McCarthyism. Young Americans of all ethnic backgrounds, who might today look to Paul Robeson as a role model for human creativity, know little or nothing of his accomplishments.

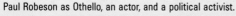

Paul Robeson as Othello, an actor, and a political activist.

With the civil rights movement, American artists and writers could no longer get away with vicious racist stereotypes.

86

March on Washington, 1963.

FREEDOM'S MARCH

Throughout the nation's history, Americans of African descent have suffered lives marked by discrimination and hardship. Millions of slaves endured incalculable suffering from their entry into the American Colonies in the 1600s to the abolition of slavery by the 13th Amendment of the Constitution in 1865. In 1868, the 14th Amendment finally gave black men full citizenship and promised them equal protection under the law.

Despite some immediate gains in the aftermath of the Civil War, the legal and political rights of African Americans declined dramatically after federal troops withdrew from the South, returning it to local white rule. Dismal economic conditions of sharecropping made life little better than it had been under slavery. Many freed blacks also found themselves the victims of terror by lynching, rape and brutal assault. Throughout the latter part of the 19th century, denial of their rights was legally sanctioned by a series of racist statutes based on the theory of white supremacy.

Known as "Jim Crow" laws, a derisive slang term for black men, these laws established different rules for blacks and whites. These laws promoted and institutionalized racial segregation, in all phases of life from birth to death, including hospitals, orphanages, schools, public transportation, hotels and restaurants, recreational facilities, and burial grounds. Signs marked "Whites Only" and "Colored" prevailed throughout the region. This legalized racism found support in a series of Supreme Court decisions in the late 19th century, including *Plessy v. Ferguson*.

The reality was that facilities for blacks were separate, but completely unequal. Racial discrimination dominated overtly in the South and more subtly in other geographic regions. Jim Crow laws were only part of the problem facing African Americans. Unwritten rules barred them from many jobs and commercial establishments. Ku Klux Klan violence kept them "in their place." Following World War I, race riots ignited throughout the United States, frequently directed against returning black soldiers. African American groups and individuals fought back, creating civil rights organizations to publicize racial violence discrimination and to seek relief in legislatures, courts and elsewhere. Still, new Jim Crow laws were enacted and economic and political rights for blacks were minimal throughout the 1920s and 30s.

The aftermath of World War II catalyzed some deeper changes in American race relations, bringing social reality more into line with constitutional ideals. By 1948, President Truman had taken measures to promote racial equality, urging Congress to enforce fair voting, hiring and transportation practices throughout the country. As Commander in Chief, Truman also ordered the complete integration of the armed forces. Many called for more action from the President and Congress, but strong southern political resistance proved a powerful block.

Support CORE Sit-Ins

Dr. King addresses
March on Washington
crowd.

March on Washington for Jobs & Freedom — August 28, 1963

200,000 TAKE PART IN CAPITAL MARCH

Negroes and White Sympathizers Demand Across-the-Board End of Discrimination

WASHINGTON (AP) — In a great, dramatic demonstration, more than 200,000 Negroes and white sym
pathizers massed before the Abraham Lincoln Me
morial Wednesday and demanded across-the-boar
abolition of race discrimination.

THE VIET CONG NEVER CALLED ME A NIGGER

Thousands of Ku Klux Klan
marchers in Washington D.C.,
circa 1920s.

By the 1950s, civil rights activities accelerated, heralding profound changes in American law and society. The Eisenhower Administration downplayed new measures to promote racial equality, forcing civil rights groups to turn to the courts to redress legitimate grievances. In 1950, the National Association for the Advancement of Colored People mounted a legal assault on educational segregation, challenging the "separate but equal" doctrine. Winning some key decisions concerning discrimination in higher education, the NAACP soon focused on segregated public schools. On May 17, 1954, the Supreme Court ruled unanimously in its favor, holding that separate educational facilities are "inherently unequal," violating the 14th Amendment equal protection clause. *Brown v. Board of Education* was a landmark decision and a signal victory for civil rights forces in the United States. The case overruled the "separate but equal" doctrine and stimulated a generation of massive social protests and activism on behalf of racial justice.

The opening battle occurred in December, 1955, in Montgomery, Alabama, when Rosa Parks refused to relinquish her bus seat to a white passenger. Jailed for her defiant act, she sparked a successful black boycott of the city bus system. Mobilized by experienced black labor leaders and women community organizers, the demonstrations were soon led by Dr. Martin Luther King, Jr., who advocated non-violent resistance to unlawful authority. Influenced by the writings of Thoreau and Gandhi, King conceived a strategy of civil disobedience to compel authorities to implement the human rights guaranteed 90 years earlier by the 13th and 14th amendments.

Social protest soon became a daily reality in the segregated South. Black student sit-in demonstrations began in Greensboro, North Carolina in February, 1960, to demand equal service from a Woolworth lunch counter. The sit-in movement spread rapidly; by April, 50,000 people had participated in sit-ins or support demonstrations in 100 southern cities and towns. More than 3,000 persons were arrested, as the nation watched with interest and anxiety. Freedom riders organized by the

Congress of Racial Equality took buses into Georgia and Alabama, seeking to integrate waiting rooms, lunch counters, public restrooms and drinking fountains. Regularly met by mob violence and police brutality, hundreds of freedom riders were beaten and jailed.

New, more militant civil rights organizations like the Student Non-violent Coordinating Committee entered the arena of public protest. Young blacks and increasing numbers of northern white supporters moved into African American communities throughout the deep South, organizing demonstrations, teaching in "Freedom Schools," and registering voters. Their activities prompted harassment in arrests, violence, and occasionally even death. The motto of the era was "putting your body on the line."

In August 1963, civil rights leaders organized a massive march on Washington, culminating in a rally of more than 250,000 people demanding jobs, freedom and full implementation of constitutional rights for racial minorities. Dr. King's stirring "I Have a Dream" speech inspired thousands of new civil rights advocates to work vigorously for these goals. The political impact of these efforts was obvious. Still facing strong resistance from southern democrats, a reluctant President John F. Kennedy finally proposed comprehensive civil rights legislation to Congress, admitting privately to civil rights leaders that street protests had forced his hand. Soon after Kennedy's assassination in November, 1963, Congress enacted landmark civil rights legislation with the strong support of the new president Lyndon Johnson.

Norman Rockwell cover of U.S. Marshals escorting school girl into a previously segregated school.

Cases and Controversies

Brown v. Board of Education (1954)

On May 17, 1954, the Supreme Court's nine Justices announced their unanimous decision in the four cases grouped together and known as *Brown v. Board of Education*. This case was one of the most important in the 20th century, a landmark ruling that segregation of children in public schools, authorized or required by state law, violated the 14th Amendment guarantee of equal protection of the law. Speaking for the Court, Chief Justice Earl Warren relied on modern scientific evidence in concluding that school segregation produced feelings of inferiority in black children, reducing their motivation to learn. Warren and his colleagues held, accordingly, that segregated educational facilities are inherently unequal.

The *Brown* decision was a political triumph as much as a major departure from existing legal doctrine. The Court was particularly sensitive to the political implications of its decision when the case was first argued in 1952. Historical evidence suggests that the Court was seriously divided. Several Justices were concerned about the probable reaction of violence and civil disorder among white Southerners if the Court ruled school segregation unconstitutional. Chief Justice Fred Vinson, who had written earlier opinions striking down segregation in universities, appeared reluctant to extend those opinions to the public schools.

Vinson died in 1953 before a final decision in the case. His replacement, California Governor Earl Warren, had the opposite view. He was determined to overturn "separate but equal" doctrine and equally determined to orchestrate a unanimous decision in a case of such politi-

cal magnitude. With the assistance of Justice Felix Frankfurter, the new Chief Justice used his considerable political skills to accomplish this goal.

For all its historical and constitutional significance in declaring equal educational opportunity, the *Brown* decision was deliberately limited in language and scope. The Supreme Court issued no orders to the defendant school boards on when they should end their segregated practices. Instead, the Court waited a full year before becoming more specific.

In its clarifying decision, sometimes called *Brown v. Board of Education* II, the Court required school boards to "make a prompt and reasonable start" toward compliance. It directed the lower courts to issue orders to schools to admit black children "with all deliberate speed." Such language reflected a concern for the political realities of the time. A common response to the Court's decision was outright defiance and evasion. Only later would the promise of the *Brown* decision become a reality. Yet, throughout the next 20 years, *Brown* served as precedent to end segregation on public transportation, recreational facilities, court houses, housing and virtually every other public institution. The decision was the critical catalyst for the momentous civil rights activities that forever changed race relations in America.

Angry whites jeer Elizabeth Eckford as she tries to attend segregated high school in Little Rock, Arkansas, 1957.

The Civil Rights Law of 1964 enforced the right to vote, authorized the government to bring suit to protect equal access and use of public facilities and education, and established a Fair Employment Practices Commission. The Voting Rights Act of 1965 suspended literacy and other voter tests that had been used for decades to disenfranchise African American citizens. It also authorized federal supervision of voter registration in states with demonstrable records of racial discrimination in the electoral process. Together, these laws expanded the role of the national government as a guarantor of civil rights, providing new legal "muscle" to implement existing constitutional rights.

The peak of federal legislative activity was accompanied by even more social protest and civil unrest. Demonstrations occurred in the North as well as the South, because African Americans in urban ghettos still lived in massive poverty, despair, and *de facto* segregation, despite their newly acquired legislative rights. The confrontational mood of the mid-1960s was stimulated by the emergence of the "Black Power" movement, influenced by the ideas of historical and contemporary radical black leaders like W.E.B. DuBois, Marcus Garvey, Paul Robeson, Malcolm X, Stokely Carmichael, Huey Newton and others.

The gains of the civil rights movement from the mid-50s to the early 70s encouraged other groups to fight with equal vigor for political and judicial recognition of their own rights. The Women's Liberation movement developed in the 60s and 70s. Led by Bella Abzug, Gloria Steinem and Betty Freidan, this prompted a newly proposed constitutional amendment: the equal rights amendment. Though not ratified, it served as a rallying point to assure women full participation in society.

Latino activists, especially in the Southwest, also organized and pressed for change. In one example, Cesar Chavez led a movement to assure better treatment and economic benefits for the thousands of migrant farmworkers. Others pressed for greater representation in state and Federal Government.

OXFORD, Miss. (AP)—Hordes of combat-ready troops clamped rigid control on this seething southern town Monday night after the enrollment of James Meredith, a Negro, ended segregation at the University of Mississippi.

Native Americans from throughout the country became effective advocates for better education and greater recognition of their unique cultures. They also fought for more autonomy and political participation in running their own affairs.

Asian Americans fought for an end to discriminatory immigration practices and redress of past wrongs such as those that arose from the Japanese Internment during World War II.

Disabled Americans pressed for fundamental changes in how society treats those with special needs. They promoted awareness for and equal access to public facilities, better special education programs and medical reform.

Gays and lesbians organized to repeal discriminatory legislation, to forbid unfair hiring practices and to change public perceptions of sexual orientation. With the tragedy of AIDS in the 1980s and 1990s, the movement also rallied to assure adequate medical research and organized collective efforts to fight the disease.

All of the movements, like the early civil rights cause, have met with resistance. Many have provoked major controversies; others have provoked a reaction on the part of majority Americans. They have met with the claim that radical social change has come too fast or has gone too far. Some have met resistance on the basis of moral or religious beliefs. Yet all of these movements demonstrate that the doctrines contained in the Bill of Rights are not absolute. While great disparities still exist in the United States, perhaps the ultimate significance of the Bill of Rights emerges when people, not just lawyers, judges and politicians, assume responsibility for determining and implementing its meaning.

Thurgood Marshall

Few blacks born in 1908 could aspire to a career as a lawyer, much less as a member of the United States Supreme Court. Great grandson of a slave and son of a Pullman steward, Thurgood Marshall became a dramatic exception to the modest expectations of black Americans in the early part of the 20th century. He was born in Baltimore and attended segregated schools as a boy. After graduating from the historically black Howard University Law School, he began practicing in 1933. In 1938, he became chief counsel of the Legal Defense Fund of the National Association for the Advancement of Colored People.

This role would soon propel him to national prominence. The NAACP Legal Defense Fund was the key legal arm of the broader struggle for justice and civil rights. By 1950, Marshall and his legal colleagues moved into high gear on a sustained attack on segregated education at all levels. Marshall began this crusade by winning important legal victories in the Supreme Court. His efforts eliminated state practices in universities and professional schools that failed to provide equal education for African American applicants.

The biggest challenge lay ahead. Working with clients in the segregated South, Marshall was ready to attack the long standing "separate but equal" doctrine in public schools. His struggles were both legal and political. He even faced powerful internal resistance in his own organization. Many civil rights activists believed that it was premature to take on the entire system of segregated public schools. Fearing that the Supreme Court would succumb to widespread public resistance to school integration, they urged caution. Determined to proceed, Marshall carried the day.

He and his staff of lawyers worked furiously to make the most effective case. In 1952, he presented the legal argument that eventually resulted in the landmark decision of *Brown v. Board of Education* in 1954. Marshall departed from traditional legal strategy by presenting the Supreme Court with persuasive evidence from the fields of psychology and social science about the effects of segregation on school children. Still, his basic argument was that no reading of the Constitution could support segregation. This victory for African American children in the courts made Marshall a civil rights hero as well as a national figure.

In 1961, President John F. Kennedy appointed him to the U.S. Court of Appeals. In 1965, President Lyndon Johnson made him Solicitor General. Two years later, Johnson appointed Marshall to the Supreme Court, where he became the first black to occupy the position of Associate Justice. For more than twenty years, Associate Justice Thurgood Marshall voted to expand the Bill of Rights by favoring greater free expression, more restrictions on police misconduct, and increased opportunities for racial minorities, welfare recipients, and other marginal groups in American society. A long illness prompted him to retire in 1991. When asked to sum up his role as a lawyer and justice, Marshall said, "He did what he could with what he had." For those who suffered from segregation or who had little power, no one did more.

Justice Thurgood Marshall.

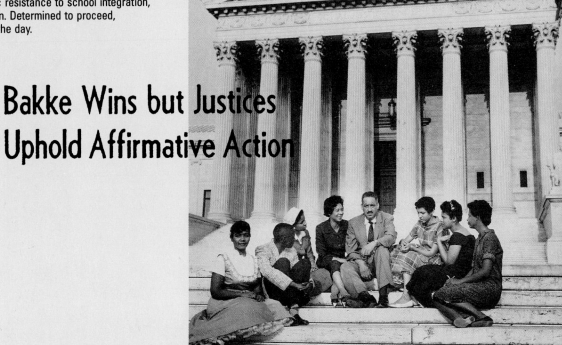

Bakke Wins but Justices Uphold Affirmative Action

Thurgood Marshall surrounded by students on steps of Supreme Court Building.

DUE PROCESS OF LAW

In 1215 Magna Carta guaranteed that Men shall only be punished according to "the Law of the Land." In 1354 Parliament recast the idea as "Due Process of Law." James Madison adopted the phrase when he wrote the Fifth Amendment and the authors of the 14th Amendment used it in their wording. The Supreme Court first interpreted due process in *Murray's Lessee v. Hoboken* (1856). The Court defined it as the settled usages and modes of proceedings in English law, "before the emigration of our ancestors," that were not unsuited to the civil and political conditions of America. Given such an elastic definition, it is no wonder that the controversy over the rights of persons charged with crimes continues to capture the attention of lawmakers, the police, the courts and the public at large.

From knotty questions of search and seizure to the right to counsel, from the right against self-incrimination to cruel and unusual punishment, volumes have been written about due process. The core issues of due process involve reconciling the legitimate needs of a society to maintain law and order and the fundamental right of every citizen to be protected from unconstitutional surveillance, arrest, conviction and punishment. Ironically, perhaps the most basic of all due process rights—that one is presumed innocent until proven guilty—appears nowhere in the Constitution or the Bill of Rights.

The Supreme Court has addressed due process questions on a case-by-case basis, applying various formulations of the "fundamental fairness" test. For example, the Court has asked whether a particular procedural safeguard is "of the very essence of a scheme of ordered liberty." Another test employed by the Court has been whether a rule or procedure is dictated by a "principle of justice so rooted in the traditions and conscience of our people as to be ranked as fundamental." Or the Court has asked whether a challenged procedure imposed by the state violated "those canons of decency and fairness which express the notions of justice of English-speaking peoples even toward those charged with the most heinous offenses." If the answer to any of these questions is "yes," the Court will invoke the due process clause of the 14th Amendment and apply it to all states.

Police arrest murder suspect in New York City.

HABEAS CORPUS: "THE GREAT WRIT OF LIBERTY"

Even before the Bill of Rights was adopted, so valued was the Writ of Habeas Corpus, that it was guaranteed in the text of the Constitution itself (Art. I, Sec. 9). Habeas Corpus is a court order commanding any official who holds someone in custody to bring that person before a court and justify the legal grounds for the restraint of personal liberty. If all else fails, Habeas Corpus serves as a last resort to gain release from illegal detention or imprisonment. Justice Felix Frankfurter wrote, "It is not the boasting of empty rhetoric that has treated the writ of habeas corpus as the basic safeguard of freedom in the Anglo-American world."

During the Civil War, when a civilian was sentenced to death by a court martial, even though the local grand jury had refused to indict him, his life was spared when the Supreme Court granted a Writ of Habeas Corpus (*Ex Parte Milligan*). And when Americans of Japanese descent, whose loyalty was unquestioned, were confined in internment camps against their will, it was a Writ of Habeas Corpus that finally won their release (*Ex Parte Endo*).

Currently, habeas corpus is most often invoked in death penalty cases. Some claim that many of these petitions are frivolous and that they bog down the courts in endless paperwork simply to delay the process. Yet, according to the American Bar Association, petitions for habeas corpus are granted in 40% of all death penalty cases. Recently, the U.S. Supreme Court showed a willingness to carefully scrutinize a second petition and deny it on the finding that the petitioner had abused the writ (*McCleskey v. Zant*, 1991).

1930s cartoon.

"Criminal Procedure!"

For example, in the 1968 case of *Duncan v. Louisiana,* the Court considered the question of whether a person accused of a misdemeanor punishable up to two years imprisonment could be denied a jury trial by state law. The Court reviewed the importance of jury trial in English and Colonial Law. It also cited the Sixth Amendment which guarantees jury trials in criminal prosecutions. The Court found that trial by jury in criminal cases is "fundamental to the American scheme of justice." Therefore, the due process clause of the 14th Amendment requires states to provide a jury trial in serious criminal cases. Because the crime charged against the defendant called for punishment "of up to two years" imprisonment, a jury trial would be required under the Sixth and Fourteenth amendments. An expanded right to jury trials taken from the Sixth Amendment had become incorporated through the 14th Amendment and made to apply to the states.

However, the Court has not always reached this result. In a later case the Court decided that a 12-person jury, though deeply rooted in English and American practice, was not fundamental. As a result, the defendant's Sixth Amendment rights were not violated when he was convicted by a six-person jury. In short, the 14th Amendment due process clause did not require a 12-person jury.

The Warren Court in the 1960s dramatically "federalized" state criminal procedures by applying federal notions of due process to the states through the 14th Amendment. More and more state criminal procedures were forced to change. In some cases, gross abuses of due process by law enforcement officials forced the Court to police the police. In a 1936 case, *Brown v. Mississippi*, a black male suspect in a murder case was beaten and tortured for hours by police before he confessed to the crime. The Court ruled that such police methods have no place in a free society and that confessions extracted under such methods are "inherently unreliable."

Unflinchingly, the Court barred the admission of illegally obtained evidence [*Mapp v. Ohio*, (1961)], and guaranteed indi-

CONTROL YOUR LOCAL POLICE

gents the right to counsel [*Gideon v. Wainwright*, (1963)]. It prohibited prosecutors from making adverse comments to the jury when a defendant exercised his constitutional right against self-incrimination by declining to take the stand [*Griffin v. California*, (1965)]. The Court guaranteed the right to confront witnesses [*Pointer v. Texas*, (1965)], and assured criminal defendants the right to use compulsory subpoenas to obtain useful evidence [*Washington v. Texas*, (1967)]. Of course, no case more stands for this judicial revolution than *Miranda v. Arizona* (1966).

These rulings required great changes in law enforcement and set off a great debate about the meaning of the Bill of Rights. Those opposed to the changes argued that by forcing states to follow these rules, the Court had upset the balance between federal and state power. Others argued that the Court was no longer merely making decisions about law, but had begun to legislate by making rules that the states or federal law enforcement officials had to follow. Aside from these arguments that the Supreme Court had tampered with the separation of powers and checks and balances in the Constitution, the Court was also accused of being unfair. Why should convicted criminals receive new trials, or reduced sentences, or, in some cases, be released, because of law enforcement errors? Others believed that the Court had gone overboard perverting the Bill of Rights to help criminals, instead of considering the victims of crimes, or their families. The legislative and executive efforts of the Reagan and Bush Administrations, and the efforts of the Justices they have appointed, sought to alter this situation. Recent decisions, without directly overruling the precedents of the Warren Court, have begun to limit their effects.

In 1990, the Court, in an opinion written by Chief Justice Rehnquist, upheld suspicionless stops and examinations of all drivers at "sobriety checkpoints" *(Michigan Department of State Police v. Sitz)*. These checkpoints seemed to be generally accepted by the public as a minor inconvenience in the fight against drug and alco-

Clarence
Earl
Gideon
and
the Right
To Counsel

Clarence Earl Gideon.

When he stole a pint of wine and a few coins from a cigarette machine at the Bay Harbor Poolroom in Panama City, Florida, Clarence Earl Gideon could not have been thinking about changing constitutional law. At his trial on August 4, 1961, Gideon made a simple request: He asked the judge to appoint a lawyer for him because he was too poor to afford one. When his request was rejected and he was convicted, Gideon appealed his case. The Florida courts upheld his conviction, so he submitted a petition to the Supreme Court, handwritten in pencil. He claimed "that all citizens tried for a felony crime should have aid of counsel." If he had been trained in the law, Gideon would have realized that all the precedents were against him. The Court had ruled that the Sixth Amendment required the appointment of counsel to all indigent *federal* criminal defendants. But, when it came to *state* criminal defendants charged with a non-capital crime, the Supreme Court had ruled in *Betts v. Brady* (1942) that a free lawyer was required only under "special circumstances." Those included illiteracy, youth, mental illness or the complexity of the charges. Gideon's case challenged that rule. The Court acknowledged Gideon's need for a lawyer to present his constitutional arguments and appointed Abe Fortas, who would later sit as a Justice of the Supreme Court. On March 18, 1963, in *Gideon v. Wainwright,* the Court overruled *Betts v. Brady* and held that Gideon had a right to counsel. Writing for the majority, Justice Hugo L. Black, who had dissented in *Betts,* declared, "The right of one charged with crime to counsel may not be deemed fundamental and essential to fair trials in some countries, but it is in ours." Gideon, a petty thief, had expanded the rights of all Americans.

"Don't worry about it! Cruel and unusual punishment applies to us if we're caught! Not to our victims!"

CRUEL AND UNUSUAL PUNISHMENT

The Eighth Amendment bans "cruel and unusual punishment." In 1958, Chief Justice Earl Warren, in *Trop v. Dulles*, wrote that these words mandated "civilized" methods of punishment compatible with "the dignity of man." The Amendment "must draw its meaning from the evolving standards of decency that mark the progress of a maturing society." In 1972, in *Furman v. Georgia*, a closely divided Supreme Court struck down all state death penalty laws because they were so lacking in clear standards that judges and juries were arbitrarily condemning people to death "wantonly and freakishly."

By 1976, Congress and thirty-five states had passed new capital punishment laws. When tested in the Supreme Court that year, those that imposed a *mandatory* death sentence for murder were struck down as repugnant to "the respect for humanity underlying the Eighth Amendment." But those that established "guided discretion" were upheld. For example, in *Gregg v. Georgia* the law required a jury to first find guilt and in a second stage to weigh "aggravating" against "mitigating" circumstances.

The Court has continued to grapple with the death penalty, outlawing mandatory execution for "cop killers" in *Roberts v. Louisiana* (1976), and prohibiting death sentences for rapists in *Coker v. Georgia* (1977). It also banned execution for the crime of felony-murder where the defendant did not participate in the murder (*Enmund v. Florida*, 1982). Yet, in many other cases, the Court has sustained the death penalty. While according to opinion polls the great majority of Americans support the death penalty, the Court will be called upon to make decisions of life and death for many years to come.

The Electric Chair.

hol abuse. Yet, in terms of our Fourth Amendment rights, *Sitz* represents the first time that the Court has authorized police searches and seizures of presumptively innocent persons for criminal law enforcement purposes, without any individualized suspicion. In dissent, Justice Stevens characterized the halting *en masse* of unsuspected ordinary citizens as one of the "hallmarks of regimes far different from ours."

In March 1991, a closely divided Court, in its 5-4 decision *Arizona v. Fulminante,* also written by Chief Justice Rehnquist, held that the admission into evidence at a criminal trial of a coerced confession would not automatically require a reversal if the court concludes that the error was "harmless." In a sharply worded dissent, Justice Bryon White and three other Justices argued that "a coerced confession is fundamentally different from other types of erroneously admitted evidence." The dissenters relied on earlier precedents for the rule that "there are some constitutional rights so basic to a fair trial that their infraction can *never* be treated as harmless error."

Ironically, the new Rehnquist Court is now itself accused by some of being an activist body, legislating rather than adjudicating. One thing is clear: debates over the essential meaning of the Bill of Rights and due process will continue.

Police officer displays Miranda Warning.

Cases and Controversies

Miranda Rights

Ernesto Miranda was arrested on charges of kidnapping and rape. He was picked out of a lineup by the victim, interrogated for several hours and then signed a confession. He had not been advised that he did not have to answer any questions or that he could have a lawyer present. The Supreme Court reversed Miranda's conviction on the grounds that the Fifth Amendment guarantees the right of a suspect to remain silent unless he chooses to speak in the "unfettered exercise of his own will." The majority opinion, written by Chief Justice Earl Warren, showed that the Court distrusted police procedures employed in a secret "interrogation environment." In *Miranda,* the Court set minimum procedures that the police must follow at the outset of interrogation. The police must clearly inform the accused of the right to remain silent, that any statement made may be used as evidence in court against the accused; that the accused has the right to the presence of an attorney; and that if the accused cannot afford an attorney, one will be appointed to represent the accused. Chief Justice Warren wrote that "[t]he warnings required and the waiver necessary in accordance with our opinion today are prerequisites to the admissibility of any statement made by a defendant." The debate over *Miranda* began immediately and persists to this day. The dissenting justices warned that the ruling weakened law enforcement and created rigid rules not required by "the more pliable dictates" of conventional due process used up to that time.

Mapp v. Ohio (1961)
Dollree Mapp and The "Exclusionary Rule"

When seven policemen appeared at her door in Cleveland, Ohio, demanding entry in search of a bomb suspect, Dollree Mapp kept them waiting while she called her lawyer. He told her to stand her ground unless they produced a search warrant. The police broke the lock, waving what they said was a "warrant" at Mapp. When she tried to read it, they grabbed it back and handcuffed her. While searching her two-story house, they happened upon a suitcase belonging to a former boarder. It contained sexual material consisting of "four little pamphlets, a couple of photographs and a little pencil doodle." Mapp was charged with possessing "lewd and lascivious" materials. Although the Ohio Supreme Court found that the evidence was "unlawfully seized during an unlawful search," it was still admissible and her conviction was upheld. But in 1961 the U.S. Supreme Court, by a 5-4 decision, held that under the Fourth Amendment the evidence should not have been used at trial. The Court had expanded the Exclusionary Rule to all state, as well as federal, crimes. Justice Tom C. Clark wrote that the Exclusionary Rule was "an essential part" of the Fourth Amendment because it deterred police from engaging in unlawful searches and seizures. "Nothing can destroy a government more quickly than its failure to observe its own laws," wrote Clark, "or worse, its disregard of the charter of its own existence."

CHAPTER 14

The First Freedom
RELIGIOUS LIBERTY IN AMERICA

The tradition of religious liberty is deeply rooted in the American experience and has served as the bedrock for the protection of other rights, including freedom of speech, press and assembly. In 1776, the Virginia Declaration of Rights guaranteed that "all men are equally entitled to the full and free exercise of religion, according to the dictates of conscience." Thomas Jefferson's Virginia Statute of Religious Liberty, adopted in 1786, stated that no person should be compelled to frequent or support any religious worship *and* that no person should suffer on account of religious opinions and beliefs.

These complementary doctrines, one prohibiting the establishment of religion by a state and the other guaranteeing the free exercise of religion, were both included in the First Amendment. They have occupied a long chapter in our constitutional history. In *Cantwell v. Connecticut* (1940), the Supreme Court said that religious liberty "embraces two concepts— freedom to believe and freedom to act. The first is absolute but, in the nature of things, the second cannot be. Conduct remains subject to regulation of society." For 200 years, the courts have tried to reconcile the conflict between the right to freely exercise and practice one's religion and the government's police powers to enact legislation for the general comfort, safety, health, morals and welfare of the citizenry at large.

In *Reynolds v. United States* (1879), the Supreme Court upheld the constitutionality of an act of Congress criminalizing polygamy on the grounds that although laws "cannot interfere with mere religious belief, they may with practice." Likewise, in *Jacobson v. Massachusetts* (1905), the Court held that compulsory vaccination against communicable diseases was enforceable regardless of religious objections. In *Prince v. Massachusetts* (1944), the Court upheld the conviction of a Jehovah's Witness for violating a child labor law by allowing her nine-year-old niece to help sell the group's religious literature on city streets.

Between 1935 and 1955, the Jehovah's Witnesses, often represented by their tenacious lawyer, Hayden Covington, won important legal victories. These cases not only enlarged religious freedom for followers of all faiths, but established vital precedents ensuring greater freedom of speech, press and assembly for everyone. Rebuffed in 1940 in *Gobitis,* the Jehovah's Witnesses successfully returned to the Supreme Court three years later in *West Virginia v. Barnette.* In that case, the Court sustained their right to refuse to salute the flag on religious grounds.

Religious diversity is part of our
Bill of Rights heritage.

In *Cantwell*, the Court held that the First Amendment guaranteed the right to teach and preach religion in the public streets and parks. While a municipal permit may be required, it could not be denied on the basis of the content of the religious teachings. Any restrictions must be applied and must be limited to time, place and manner of the speech, not to the speech itself. The same year, in *Cox v. New Hampshire*, the Court unanimously ruled that religious liberty included the right to participate in public religious processions. *Cox* would serve as a key precedent to protect civil rights demonstrators during the 1960s.

The Court first addressed the Establishment Clause in 1947 in *Everson v. Board of Education*. A sharply divided Court endorsed Jefferson's "wall of separation" between church and state. Still the Court upheld a New Jersey program that allowed local schoolboards to reimburse parents for the cost of public transportation to both public and private religious schools.

The following year, in *McCollum v. Board of Education*, the Court put meat on the bone of strict separation of church and state. It struck down Illinois' "release time" program, popular in many states. Under the program, students were excused from class to attend religious instruction given in public school buildings. Four years later in *Zorach v. Clausen* (1952), New York's release time program was upheld because the religious instruction took place on off-school premises.

In *Engel v. Vitale* (1962), the Court confronted the issue of religious prayers in the public schools. New York had offered a voluntary, non-denomination invocation of "Almighty God." In an 8-1 decision, the Court struck down the policy. It found that it is "no part of the business of government to compose official prayers for any group of the American people to recite as part of a religious program carried on by government." The following year, in *Abington v. Schempp* (1963), the Court outlawed devotional Bible reading in public schools. But the Court assured educators that nothing in the opinion prohibited the study of comparative religions or the Bible as a historical and literary work. In *Wallace v. Jaffree*

(1985), the Court invalidated an Alabama law that required a one-minute moment of silence for "meditation or voluntary prayer."

When Arkansas prohibited the teaching in its public schools "that mankind ascended or descended from a lower order of animals," the Court, in *Epperson v. Arkansas* (1968), overturned the law. The Court found that the state had "sought to prevent its teachers from discussing the theory of evolution because it is contrary to the beliefs of some that the book of Genesis must be the exclusive source of the doctrine of the origin of man."

The Court has had to decide what constitutes "religion" for protection under the First Amendment. In *Torcaso v. Watkins* (1961), the Court decided that an atheist could not be excluded from testifying in court. An exemption from the draft, for

Cases and Controversies

Wisconsin v. Yoder (1972)

In this case, three Amish families refused to send their children to high school after they finished eighth grade. The refusal violated Wisconsin's compulsory education law. Yet the Amish believed that modern secondary education violated their religious principles. In spite of their beliefs, the Amish fathers were convicted of violating Wisconsin's compulsory education law. The U.S. Supreme Court, in an opinion by Chief Justice Warren Burger, reversed the convictions. The Court took note that the beliefs of the Amish were deeply rooted and based on profound religious conviction. These beliefs required the Amish to turn their back on worldly concerns and live simply on the land. From the Amish point of view, high school took young people away from the community at a time most important for their religious development. Based on these special conditions, the Court held that the right of the children to the "free exercise" of their religion under the First Amendment outweighed the state's interest in education. In a dissent, Justice William O. Douglas argued that the decision of whether a child should not go to school on religious principles should not be left to the parents alone. He argued that the lifelong consequences of this kind of decision should not be made for children whose views differ from their parents.

William & Lillian Gobitis

Jehovah's Witnesses, William and Lillian Gobitis, ages ten and twelve, had been taught not to worship graven images. When required to say the Pledge of Allegiance at school, the children declined on the grounds that the salute was a form of forbidden idolatry. The Minersville, Pennsylvania school board expelled them. Their case reached the U.S. Supreme Court in 1940. Speaking for the majority, Justice Felix Frankfurter wrote that the children's religious beliefs did not relieve them of their civic duties. The school board was free to encourage national loyalty, "that unifying sentiment without which there can ultimately be no liberties, civil or religious." The sole dissenter, Justice Stone, wrote that "the state seeks to coerce these children to express a sentiment which . . . they do not entertain and which violates their deepest religious convictions." By failing to act in the name of "judicial restraint," the Court had achieved "no more than the surrender of the constitutional protection of the liberty of small minorities to the popular will." Three years later, the Supreme Court reversed itself in the *Barnette* case. The case of the Gobitis children, therefore, stands for more than just the principle of religious freedom against the power of the state. It also demonstrates that the Supreme Court can change its mind about what the Bill of Rights means and protects.

those who believed in a "Supreme Being," was considered in *United States v. Seeger* (1965). The Court enlarged the exemption to apply to anyone who possessed a sincere belief occupying a place in their life parallel to that filled by belief in God. Such cases demonstrate just one of the dilemmas which the Court must untangle when trying to deal with questions of religious liberty. What beliefs qualify under the First Amendment for religious protection?

When the University of Missouri attempted to abide by the Court's demand for strict separation of church and state, it barred a student religious group from meeting on the campus for religious teaching or worship. The Court, in *Widmar v. Vincent* (1981), held that having "created a forum generally open for use by student groups," the University was forbidden to violate the free speech and association rights of the religious groups. No state sponsorship of religion was implied since the University provided a forum equally open to all student groups.

In 1990, the Court issued a new decision covering religion in *Employment Division v. Smith,* known as the "Peyote Case." Federal law permits the use of peyote in Native American religious ceremonies as does that of about half the states. Oregon is not one of them. That state denied unemployment benefits to two Native American drug counselors who had been fired for

using peyote at religious rituals. Where prior Supreme Court decisions had required a state to show a "compelling interest" in order to override the free exercise of one's religion, Justice Antonin Scalia moved away from those precedents. The Court held that presuming that such regulations are invalid when applied to religious practice in a very diverse society is a "luxury" we cannot afford. The Court ruled that the free exercise of religion does not protect criminal conduct as long as the law is applied equally to all religious practice. The drug counselors' claim could be denied.

As minority religions become a greater factor in American life — Native American, Moslem, Rastafarian, Hasidim, Santerian, Evangelical, and others — with no single denomination commanding a majority, issues about the meaning of the First Amendment free exercise and establishment clauses will become more important than ever.

CHAPTER
15

A LIVING BILL OF RIGHTS

As the Bill of Rights enters a new century, the challenge for the United States is to preserve a system of individual rights in the midst of an ever more complex and often confusing world. Are there universal values reflected in the Bill of Rights, which will sustain us in new and unexpected circumstances? How much freedom can we afford? How much tolerance can we tolerate? These, and other endless and perplexing questions, no longer remain the private preserve of scholars and philosophers. Indeed they can no longer be left to our lawyers, our judges and our politicians. Instead, they press themselves upon each of us, insisting that we think about them and decide for ourselves.

Does the Bill of Rights protect the right to decline a drug test? The right to use a federal grant to display indecent art? The right to beg for money in public subways? The right of a homeless person to live in the street? The right of a college student to use racist epithets? The right to sunbathe on a public beach in the nude? The right of a newspaper to publish the name of a rape victim? The right of a doctor in a federally funded clinic to advise a pregnant teenager about abortion? The right of tobacco companies to advertise cigarettes?

Does the Bill of Rights protect the right of religious fundamentalists to organize boycotts of the sponsors of television pro-grams that portray gay lifestyles in a favorable light? The right of women and minority students to be protected from harassment on campus? The right of a reporter to keep his or her sources confidential? The right of criminal defendants to force news reporters to divulge their sources in order to prove their innocence? The right of a hunter to buy a rifle without waiting seven days? The right of a student newspaper to publish anything the *New York Times* could lawfully publish? The right of an atheist student to ban the use of prayers at commencement exercises? The right of any religious group to display its symbols on public property? The right to burn a flag? The right to burn the Bill of Rights itself?

Is the Bill of Rights up to the task of answering these questions? Do the precedents of the last 200 years adequately equip us for this task? In addressing new claims for constitutional rights, one threshold issue is whether we are bound by the intentions of the men who wrote the Bill of Rights two centuries ago. Or is the Constitution a living document, which can be reinterpreted in each generation, to adapt to changing conditions in contemporary life?

In a speech before the American Bar Association in July 1985, Attorney General Edwin Meese announced that it would be the policy of the Reagan Administration to press for a jurisprudence of "original intention." He warned against any "drift back toward the radical egalitarianism and expansive civil libertarianism of the Warren Court." To achieve

Congress taking the Oath of Office to uphold the Constitution and its Bill of Rights.

THE RIGHT TO KEEP AND BEAR ARMS

One of the most enduring constitutional debates is whether the Second Amendment guarantees the right of private citizens to own guns. The Amendment is only one sentence: "A well regulated Militia, being necessary to the security of a free State, the right of the people to keep and bear Arms, shall not be infringed." Some observers trace the Amendment to Aristotle's observation that basic to tyrants is a "mistrust of the people; hence they deprive them of arms." James Madison wrote in the *Federalist #46* that Americans need never fear the Federal Government because of "the advantage of being armed, which you possess over the people of almost every other nation."

Others argue that the Second Amendment protects only the states' right to arm their own military forces. Its purpose may be determined by its preamble which expressly refers to a "well regulated Militia." But still others point out that in the 18th century, the militia included the entire adult male citizenry. In rebuttal it is noted that such is not the case today.

While the Supreme Court has never fully interpreted the Second Amendment, virtually all courts agree that it does not prevent all gun controls. Prohibiting gun ownership by minors, felons or the mentally impaired, or banning private ownership of certain classes of weapons, such as artillery or automatic weapons, or requiring registration or waiting periods are examples of controls permitted by the Second Amendment.

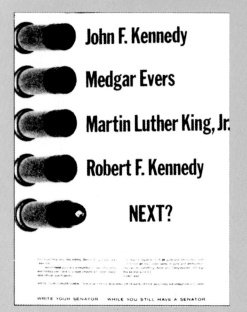

this goal, Meese argued that all constitutional issues should be decided solely on the basis of what the original Framers had intended. "In the cases we file and those we join as amicus, we will endeavor to resurrect the original meaning of constitutional provisions and statutes as the only reliable guide to judgment," he said. Meese assured his audience that the jurisprudence of original intention would produce "defensible principles of government that would not be tainted by ideological predilection."

Meese said original intent reflected "a deeply rooted commitment to the idea of democracy." By this he meant that the rule of the majority, as declared by the government, should prevail over the rights of the minority and the individual. That is, unless those rights were explicitly spelled out in the Constitution. The "only reliable guide" for interpreting the Constitution, argued Meese, is confined to the original intent in the minds of those who wrote the Constitution. If this approach were adopted, Meese presumed, the courts, exercising "judicial restraint," would defer to legislative and executive decrees and turn aside new claims of individual rights. In this way, argued Meese, the Court could avoid "legislating" from the bench and return to its role of interpreting the Constitution.

A few months later, in a speech at Georgetown University in October 1985, Associate Justice William J. Brennan rejected the "original intent" theory. It is "arrogant," Brennan claimed, "to pretend that from our vantage we can gauge accurately the intent of the Framers on application of principle to specific, contemporary questions."

Justice Brennan pointed out that the records of the constitutional debates 200 years ago were incomplete. In Brennan's view, they "provide sparse or ambiguous evidence of the original intention." He concluded that typically "all that can be gleaned is that the Framers themselves did not agree about the application or meaning of particular constitutional provisions, and hid their differences in cloaks of generality."

Robert Bork
and
The Right
Of Privacy

One debate spans the entire history of the Bill of Rights, from the arguments over its ratification 200 years ago to the Supreme Court confirmation hearings of Robert H. Bork in 1987 to the present day debates over the right of privacy. One side argues that if the Constitution is the source of our liberties, then only rights *expressly* designated in that document are free from regulation by the will of the majority. The other side might argue that we have certain inalienable rights, which pre-date the Constitution and are implied in that document.

Bork, a noted jurist and legal scholar, claimed that the Supreme Court should only recognize rights expressly found in the Constitution and the Bill of Rights. For example, Bork asserted that the right of privacy "doesn't have any rooting in the Constitution." He denounced the Supreme Court's 1965 decision in *Griswold v. Connecticut,* which struck down a law barring the use of contraceptives, even by married couples. He ridiculed the Ninth Amendment— which provides that rights not enumerated in the Constitution are nevertheless "retained by the people"—as a "waterblot on the Constitution" with no real meaning.

The right of privacy is the label often given to that collection of un-enumerated rights which are beyond government interference. Was Bork correct when he describes the right of privacy as a "free-floating right that was not derived in a principled fashion from constitutional materials?"

The right to privacy is not specifically mentioned in the constitution. Yet, the Supreme Court has recognized the right of personal privacy in its cases, most notably in the landmark case of *Roe v. Wade*. The Court mentioned the First, Fourth, Fifth, Ninth and Fourteenth amendments as containing the roots of a right to privacy. It held that these roots give a woman the right to have an abortion, at least in the first three months of pregnancy, without governmental interference.

By claiming that the Supreme Court erred in finding a constitutional issue for privacy, Bork thrust himself into the most controversial of constitutional issues and social debates. The Senate Judiciary committee rejected Bork's nomination to the Supreme Court, deciding that his views about privacy and other un-enumerated rights were at odds ". . . with the history of the Supreme Court in building our tradition of constitutionalism."

While Robert Bork lost his chance to become a Justice of the Supreme Court, his words renewed Constitutional debate on these issues. It remains to be seen if his ideas will find expression in future decisions of the Court.

The Warren Court, 1955.

Supreme Court nominee, Robert Bork, testifying before Senate Judiciary Committee.

Obscenity, Mapplethorpe And 2 Live Crew

Since 1973, the Supreme Court has upheld obscenity laws which comply with a three-part test adopted in *Miller v. California*. The prosecution must prove, beyond a reasonable doubt, that "the average person, applying contemporary standards" would find that the work, taken as whole, appeals to the "prurient interest . . . ." It must also prove that the work depicts or describes, in a patently offensive way, sexual conduct specifically defined by the applicable state law. Finally the prosecution must prove that the work, taken as a whole, lacks serious literary, artistic, political, or scientific value.

For the first time in American history, on April 7, 1990, an art museum was indicted for obscenity. The Cincinnati Contemporary Arts Center had just opened "The Perfect Moment," an exhibit of 175 photographs by the late Robert Mapplethorpe, a renowned photographer. In 1984 the National Endowment for the Arts had awarded Mapplethorpe a fellowship. In 1988 the NEA paid to help mount the show. The trial began on September 24, 1990. At stake were 7 of the 175 Mapplethorpe photographs. All were part of a special portion of the exhibit from which children had been excluded. Five were graphic depictions of homo-eroticism and the other two were photographs of young children in various states of nudity.

The prosecutor's entire case in chief was to present the photographs to the jury. He asked: "You have the chance to decide on your own — where do you draw the line? Are these the kinds of pictures that should be permitted in the museum?" By contrast, the defense put on an elaborate series of expert witnesses testifying to the artistic merit of the Mapplethorpe exhibit. The defense urged the jurors "to show the country that this is a community of tolerant and sensitive people." The prosecutor appealed to a different sense of civic pride. He urged them to let the world know that Cincinnati was different from other cities. On October 5, 1990, the eight-person jury, after only three hours of deliberation, found the Arts Center not guilty on all charges. "The prosecution basically decided to show us the pictures so that we'd say they weren't art when everybody else was telling us they were," said one juror. "The defendants were innocent until proven guilty, and they didn't prove them guilty."

Meanwhile, across the country in Fort Lauderdale, Florida, other First Amendment decisions were being made. On October 2, 1990, Charles Freedman, a record store owner, was convicted of selling the notorious 2 Live Crew album *As Nasty As They Wanna Be*. On October 20, 1990, in a separate prosecution, the group itself was acquitted for performing several songs from the same album at a nightclub. 2 Live Crew's lyrics contain explicit sexual references and portray women as objects to be sexually dominated. Yet, one of the defendant's expert witnesses, Henry L. Gates, then a professor of literature at Duke University, called the music "astonishing and refreshing."

The prosecutor of the case and his witnesses saw things differently. His argument held that the lyrics were not only legally obscene, but potentially dangerous. That is, they could prompt sex crimes against women or children.

In the trial against the 2 Live Crew, the jury disagreed with the prosecutor. One juror put it this way: "You take away one freedom, and pretty soon they're all gone."

The conviction against the record store owner is being appealed. Both cases stand for the principle that decisions about obscenity and the First Amendment will always be a matter of heated debate.

Censorship protester at Mapplethorpe Exhibit, Cincinnati, Ohio.

"We need more bluecoats and fewer bluenoses."

Police burn obscene
literature, 1935.

Art supporters demonstrate in
favor of federal funding for
the arts.

Justice Brennan pointed out another problem he had with original intent when he asked "[w]hose intention is relevant—that of the drafters, the congressional disputants, or the ratifiers in the states?" There were 55 delegates to the Philadelphia Convention, but only 38 signed the document on September 17, 1787. Some delegates helped draft certain provisions, but did not approve the final charter. Are their intentions relevant in interpreting those certain provisions? The entire document?

There were 1,648 delegates to the various state ratifying conventions spanning the period from 1787 to 1790. Roughly two-thirds of them voted in favor of the Constitution, but others held out for amendments that later became the Bill of Rights. Even if the diaries of each of these ratifiers were unearthed, would the meaning of the Constitution or the Bill of Rights depend on what they say they intended?

The Constitution has been amended 16 times since 1791, most notably after the Civil War. What of the intentions of those in Congress and the states who adopted and ratified those amendments? Are they relevant? The very fact that the Constitution has been amended means that the intentions of the original draftsmen cannot serve as the "only" basis for constitutional interpretation.

Rust v. Sullivan (1991)
Public Funds And Freedom Of Speech

On May 23, 1991, the Supreme Court issued a closely divided 5-4 decision in the case of *Rust v. Sullivan*. It upheld a Federal regulation that prohibited doctors and other health care providers, in publicly funded clinics, from advising pregnant women about the option of abortion. If a patient asked about abortion, the regulations required doctors to say that "the project does not consider abortion an appropriate method of family planning." The doctor's actual medical opinion did not matter. A coalition of women's rights groups, medical groups and civil libertarians challenged the regulations. They argued that the regulations were a direct violation of the physician's freedom of expression and the doctor-patient relationship. They also argued that the regulations placed an unconstitutional burden on a women's right to choose abortion.

The majority opinion, by Chief Justice Rehnquist, rejected these arguments. The opinion held that since the clinics are funded by government money, the government could encourage childbirth over abortion, without

Both sides of the abortion debate face-off marking the 17th anniversary of the *Roe* decision.

violating the Constitution. The dissenting opinion, by Justice Blackmun, warned that "Until today, the Court never has upheld viewpoint-based suppression of speech simply because that suppression was a condition upon the acceptance of public funds."

Rust also held that the freedom of speech of public employees on the job could be restricted, so long as they were free to express themselves on their own time. Citing a series of precedents spanning the last quarter-century, the dissenters found that it was "beyond question" that "a government may not require an individual to relinquish rights guaranteed him by the First Amendment as a condition of public employment."

Given widespread public funding at federal, state and local levels, *Rust* could represent a marked change in First Amendment law. It could expand the power of government to control free speech in any activity supported with public funds.

It may also serve as the beginning of a new era of constitutional law. Some argue that given recent decisions such as *Rust* and new appointments, the Supreme Court can no longer be counted on as the primary caretaker of individual rights. This may shift the battle over rights to state courts, Congress and state legislatures. If this is true, the long-term implications for the Bill of Rights will engage the American people well into the 21st century.

Justice Brennan concluded by observing that sole reliance on original intent "is a choice no less political than any other; it expresses antipathy to claims of the minority rights against the majority." If confined by the 18th century social and political attitudes of the Framers, then women, blacks and Native Americans could never achieve the "Blessings of Liberty." "Those who would restrict claims of right to the values of 1789," Justice Brennan urged, "turn a blind eye to social progress and . . . to changes of social circumstance." Justice Brennan's rejection of original intent did not settle the issue. Though many legal experts agree that the idea of original intent as the primary guide for interpreting the Constitution is too restrictive, the question remains: What should the Supreme Court use?

Justice Holmes may have best addressed the question more than 70 years ago when he wrote that the words of the Constitution "have called into being a life the development of which could not have been foreseen completely by the most gifted of its begetters . . . . The case before us must be considered in the light of our whole experience and not merely in that of what was said [two] hundred years ago."

Chinese students and their symbol of liberty against oppression, "The Goddess of Democracy."

FOUNDATIONS of FREEDOM

The Huntington Library. The original manuscripts, rare books and other documents presented in *Foundations of Freedom* represent only a very small part of the highly important American historical collections at the Huntington Library of San Marino, California. The Library is a research institution for the scholarly study of British and American history and literature. The Library Exhibition Hall, as well as the Huntington's notable Art Collections and the Botanical Gardens, are open to the public.

The W.M. Keck Foundation, one of the nation's largest foundations in terms of total annual grants, primarily supports accredited universities and colleges throughout the United States in the sciences, engineering and medical research. It also supports programs serving Southern California in the areas of community services, health care, precollegiate education, and the arts.

Constitutional Rights Foundation is a non-profit, non-partisan organization with a 29-year history of bringing citizenship education programs and materials in the areas of law and government, business and citizen participation to our nation's classrooms. Marshall Croddy, the Director of Program and Materials Development, is a lawyer and educator who has developed, written and edited numerous publications on law and the Constitution.

John H. Rhodehamel is Archivist of American Historical Manuscripts and Curator of the Huntington Library's exhibition "The Sacred Fire of Liberty: Creation of the American Bill of Rights," marking the Bicentennial of the Bill of Rights with the Henry E. Huntington Library, San Marino, California. Previously, he served as Archivist at Mount Vernon.

Stephen F. Rohde, a graduate of Northwestern University and Columbia Law School, is a constitutional lawyer, lecturer and author. He is Co-chair of the Los Angeles County Bar Association Bill of Rights Bicentennial Committee and Guest Editor of a special issue of the Beverly Hills Bar Association Journal devoted to the Bill of Rights.

Paul Von Blum, a member of the California Bar, has taught at the University of California for 22 years. At present, he teaches in the Center for Afro-American Studies at UCLA. Since 1990, he has also been a visiting faculty member in political science at the University of California at Irvine. He is the author of numerous books and articles on politics, history and culture.

BICENTENNIAL